The
IS MANAGEMENT SERIES volume 1

IT AT THE HEART OF BUSINESS

THE BRITISH COMPUTER SOCIETY

IT AT THE HEART OF BUSINESS

The British Computer Society, 1 Sanford Street, Swindon, Wiltshire SN1 1HJ

ISBN 1-902505-26-3

British Cataloguing in Publication Data
A CIP catalogue record for this book is available from the British Library

First Printed in September 2000
Printed & bound in the UK by The Charlesworth Group

Acknowledgement

Guy Fitzgerald and the authors would like to thank all those who have made this book possible, particularly the people in the companies who gave up their time to be interviewed, told their stories so eloquently, and patiently answered our questions.

Executive Summary

This book contains three real-world case studies of companies that have been particularly successful in the management and use of IT in their organisations. The three companies are winners of the **British Computer Society – Information Systems Management Awards** for the last three years. They have each, in their own ways, used and managed IT to make major impacts and contributions to their respective businesses. The case studies illustrate the development and progress of the projects from the perspective of those who made them happen. They provide rich insights not normally available except to those actively involved.

The first case is the **London Ambulance Service's – Computer Aided Dispatch (CAD) system**. The London Ambulance Service is perhaps better known for its notorious CAD system failure in 1992, this hit the headlines and entered the nation's psyche as an IT disaster. What is less well known is that the London Ambulance Service has worked very hard since that time, in a very adverse environment, to turn that failure into a shining success. The case study provides the insight in to how this remarkable feat was achieved.

The second case study is that of the **Halifax Share Dealing Service**. As is well known the Halifax, the UKs biggest building society, converted to public limited company status in 1997 and became a bank, with 8 million members benefiting from the allocation of free shares. Amidst the enormous demands of conversion the Halifax took the opportunity to re-engineer traditional industry processes and build a totally new, IT enabled, share dealing business. They turned what would have been a £9 million cost into a £6 million profit as well as providing an internet and telephone based all-share dealing facility for the company.

The third case study The **Automobile Association**'s system that helped turn around the traditional roadside rescue and repair organisation. The AA was facing increasing and intensive competition, particularly from new entrants to the industry. Typically these new entrants did not incur the costs of owning and managing a national breakdown fleet and were competing effectively by deploying existing local garage-based breakdown facilities. The AA responded to this threat by introducing a radically new command and control system – **AAHELP**. This served to enhance their existing strengths, by cutting average waiting times by 30%, dramatically improving their customer satisfaction, as well as providing a range of longer-term strategic benefits.

These case studies, although all technologically based, highlight the importance of the traditional virtues of effective management. Technology is a crucial enabler but it is not enough. The key difference, the thing that sets apart success from failure, is the way these projects are organised and managed. A relevant lesson that befits the winners of an award that focuses on the 'management' of information systems.

The cases themselves are full of issues and lessons for the reader to extract depending on their particular interests and experiences. At the end of each case the authors highlight the lessons and issues that emerged for them as well as identifying some of the common features from all three cases.

Professor Guy Fitzgerald, Brunel University

Introduction

This book outlines the case studies of three companies that have displayed excellence in information systems management. Their achievements have all been recognised as winners of the prodigious **British Computer Society – IS Management Awards.**

To win the award the company has to prove themselves excellent in the management of information systems in three major categories:

- The impact of information systems on the performance of the organisation.
- The quality of the relationships with customers, users and systems providers.
- Management of the development and/or operation of the system

The Awards have been presented annually since 1992. During this period many significant business achievements through IT have been recognised. Whilst a certain amount of publicity ensues for the winning project generally, the detail of the winning projects and what made them excellent is all too quickly forgotten and the opportunity of learning from such exemplars is lost. This year it was decided to try to capture the detail of these case studies so that a wider readership could understand and potentially draw lessons from the experiences.

The BCS felt that this would also be beneficial for the Awards scheme itself, for the winners, but most of all for the IS professional community at large. There are many excellent IS projects out there, most of them do not win awards nor receive the plaudits that they deserve, but equally there are some IS failures and projects that do not live up to expectation. Unfortunately, the failures often receive more publicity than the successes and the general perception is that the failures dominate the successes. This is not true and we hope that this book will be a small contribution to changing that balance and that examination of these success stories will help others to also be successful.

The BCS commissioned Guy Fitzgerald and his colleagues at Brunel University to undertake the task of drawing together this material. For this first edition, of what is hoped to be an annual volume, it was decided to research and publish the case studies of the last three winners from 1997 – 1999. These include:

- **London Ambulance Service – CAD (Computer Aided Dispatch) System**, 1997 winner.
- **Halifax Share Dealing Service**, 1998 winner.
- **AAHELP (The Automobile Association)**, 1999 winner.

Guy Fitzgerald and his team interviewed the major players in each of these case studies to produce this enlightening insight into the major impact IT has had on all three organisations. The cases highlight the three vital areas: impact on performance, quality of relationships and management.

The BCS Information Systems Management Awards

The BCS IS Management Awards recognise achievement, improvement, and innovation in the management of Information Systems.

Submissions receive an initial review, before being reviewed more thoroughly by an assessment panel, whose members are chosen for their broad based experience and knowledge of effective use of Information Systems. Panel member visits follow during the first three months of the year, and a shortlist of three finalists is then prepared. All organisations selected for assessment receive a comprehensive feedback report. The three finalists are invited to make a presentation to a judging panel of senior business executives from the public and private sectors and academics. The Awards are presented at a prestige dinner held in May each year.
Nominations may either refer to: programmes which have come to fruition where measurable achievement can be demonstrated, or to: continuous long-term programmes where initial and estimated benefits can be shown. Nominations must relate to the work of a team and may be made by those involved or by a third party.

The BCS IS Management Award is sponsored by Blue Circle Industries, Deloitte & Touche, The Impact Programme, Unisys, and Woolwich, and is run in association with the Financial Times.

Contributors

Managing Editor: Guy Fitzgerald

Guy Fitzgerald is Professor of Information Systems at Brunel University and Deputy Head of the Department of Information Systems and Computing. Prior to this he was the Cable & Wireless Professor of Business Information Systems at Birkbeck College, University of London. He has also worked in the computer industry with companies such as British Telecom, Mitsubishi and CACI Inc, International.

His research interests are concerned with the management and development of information systems and he has published widely in these areas. He is co-author of a major text entitled Information Systems Development: Methodologies, Techniques and Tools, and he is founder and co-editor of the Information Systems Journal (ISJ) from Blackwell Science. He combines academic and consulting activities and is passionate about ensuring the effective use of IT within businesses.

Other contributors

Lynne Baldwin is a lecturer in the Department of Information Systems and Computing at Brunel University. She is the Undergraduate Director and also the Assistant Head of Department for Learning and Teaching. She received an MA in Language and Communication from the University of East Anglia. Her research interests are varied, although there is a strong emphasis on knowledge management, decision-making, and related communication issues in both industry and educational settings.

Ela Klecun-Dabrowska is a lecturer in Information Systems at Brunel University. She obtained a degree in Computing from London Guildhall University. She holds a Masters in Analysis, Design and Management of Information Systems from the London School of Economics, where she is currently registered for a Ph.D., having secured sponsorship from BT. Her research interests include telehealth (the use of information and communication technologies in health care), evaluation of information systems, and systems analysis and design methodologies. Before becoming a lecturer she worked as an analyst/programmer for a software house.

Feroz Siddiqui holds a BSc (Hons.) degree in Business & Computer Studies and an MSc degree in Information Systems, both from Brunel University. He is currently undertaking a PhD in Information Systems, also at Brunel University. His research is concerned with flexibility in information systems and the research title is 'An Investigation of Flexibility in the Object-Oriented Paradigm'.

He has additional research interests in the area of Business Engineering, including Business Process Re-engineering, Continuous Process Improvement and Convergent Engineering. He also works as a freelance Systems Developer and IT Consultant for a number of small organisations.

Contents

Chapter 1

AA (The Automobile Association)

1.1 Introduction

The AA markets itself as 'the fourth emergency service' and this gives a flavour of its core business, that is, providing roadside assistance to its nine million plus members. Its importance in the UK is demonstrated by the fact that one in three of all UK motorists belongs to the AA, although in an increasingly competitive market, its rivals are keen to ensure a greater presence. Of note is that the AA is not only a market leader in the UK, but also that it has the world's largest patrol force. The task of the patrol force, numbering some 3,600, is to go to the aid of AA members who have broken down as quickly as possible. The yellow vans of the patrol force are equipped to repair the vehicle but also a means of communicating with colleagues who have earlier taken the call from the member who has broken down. Once at the scene of the breakdown, the patrol repairs over 80% of the jobs. The size of the task for the AA is demonstrated by the fact that the nationwide network of centres, which handles all the incoming calls from members who have broken down and need assistance, numbers six million calls a year, around 16,500 a day. Members call, at no cost, one telephone number, and are automatically put through to the nearest call centre, where the breakdown call is passed to the first available operator, the call handler, by an automatic call distribution system. In order to support the business of the call handler taking the breakdown call and getting a patrol to the member (or assisting the member in other ways) the AA uses a PC-based system known as AAHELP. It is this system that was the basis of their winning the BCS Award in 1999. AAHELP involved an investment of £35 million and its development, and subsequent benefits to the organisation, are detailed in the following sections. However, as with all information systems, it is important not to lose sight of the context in which it is developed. This introduction will therefore provide a brief history of the AA and the business context in which it now operates.

Of central importance to the AA are its members, the motorists, and since its inception in 1905, the first words of its current overview of the company, 'From pushbike to the fourth emergency service', 'courtesy and care have been the watchwords' of the business. Formed initially to help motorists avoid police speed traps aimed at catching reckless drivers (travelling, in those days at less than 20 miles per hour!) AA patrols cycled up and down the London to Brighton road at weekends. When these 'scouts' spied a speed trap, they warned drivers and thus prevented them from being arrested for speeding, although this action in turn led to AA patrols being prosecuted themselves for obstructing the police in their duties. As a courtesy AA patrols at that time saluted passing members. In order to avoid prosecution patrols were instructed not to salute if a police trap was in the vicinity. Since then, the AA has steadily developed the range of services it offers to its members to become the premier motorists' assistance organisation it is today.

The AA faces increasing competition. In addition to the other well-known breakdown service organisations such as the RAC, there are also many new players. These are smaller organisations offering roadside help, like Green Flag (bought by Direct Line), which grew from a local base but are now becoming much more visible nationally. These smaller operators do not usually own their own fleets of patrol vans but instead rely on garages to provide roadside assistance. This fact is central to the AA in that it has its own patrols who are equipped to ensure that the majority of repairs are carried out at the roadside rather than at its approved garages. The AA argues that roadside repair means that members are back on the road again more quickly and at reduced cost and inconvenience. In addition to these newer, smaller companies, insurance companies, among others, are increasingly becoming interested in providing a breakdown service themselves rather than through organisations such as the AA. During the early 1990s the AA's market dominance was eroded as competitors used technology to get to their members quickly, rivalling the response times of the AA. However, simple response time, that is, time to get to the member, is not the only, or even the best, measure of service. Getting the member back on the road again can be argued to be a more important performance measure, and one in which the AA with its own patrols and roadside repair ability feels that it excels. Nevertheless it is important for the AA to match, or better, their rivals in terms of response times.

Before 1950, AA patrols were using dedicated AA and post office telephone call boxes, which members could use to telephone for assistance. In 1950 the AA deployed mobile radio (AM), which allowed the patrols to be contacted more easily. Even today, the AA network has a better national coverage than other mobile providers. 1970 saw the first of a network of operations centres which was completed in 1990, bringing the number of centres to eight in total. During the 1980s, a predecessor of AAHELP, Command and Control was implemented. The system used computers, radios and mobile data terminals and by 1986 it was implemented across seven operations centres. In 1990 there were 500 terminals, 3,600 MDTs (Mobile Data Terminals) in patrol vehicles and eight ICL mainframes. A year before this, FM radio replaced AM. These changes might be seen more as incremental in nature, which makes the implementation of AAHELP all the more radical. AAHELP was initiated in 1992, and is a generic system that was designed to support all of the AA's service delivery processes. This system has delivered not just quicker response times for the patrol getting to the member, but also better resource planning. This in turn has led to more cars being repaired by the roadside rather than being towed or relayed, as well as better management of the breakdown situation itself. The system has also delivered major operational savings and improved customer satisfaction and, importantly, AAHELP has proved vital in maintaining the AA's market leadership. Not only was AAHELP a major investment (at £35 million) but it also revolutionised the organisation in many ways, as will be seen from further sections in this chapter. What now follows is a description of AAHELP itself, its design and implementation and its benefits to the organisation. The chapter concludes by drawing together the aspects that were instrumental in its success which, seen against the backdrop of the much-reported spectacular failure of so many IS/IT systems in the 1980s and 1990s, makes the experience of the development of AAHELP of great interest.

1.2 The AAHELP system

The previous Command and Control system provided automated call handling and enabled staff to manually deploy patrols to members. Dispatchers were responsible for deployment, that is, sending patrols to members, and they made decisions regarding the way each job (breakdown) should be dealt with. They would therefore decide whether the job required sending to a particular patrol or whether it should instead be referred to a garage agent. A number of factors had to be taken into consideration in any particular case: the nature of the breakdown, the resources available, and their geographical location. As with any system, central to its success and operation was not only the technology but the people involved; and a strong personal bond was formed, via the radio, between the dispatcher and the patrol. In addition to these personal, factors, overall management of resources demanded that breakdown patterns (daily peaks in demand), weather patterns, and the most efficient way of utilising patrols had to be taken into consideration. As well as the concern that no members had to wait an unacceptable length of time, thus maintaining service levels at an acceptable economic rate per member.

1.2.1 Command and Control

The Command and Control system was successful. It met business needs, including reduction of costs, improved quality and speed of response, better management information and customer care. Why, then, introduce AAHELP ? The importance of dispatch to the business was widely recognised, yet this was identified as a bottleneck. The system was inflexible and costly to change. It lacked resilience, having monolithic software and hardware. The hardware was approaching the end of its useful life. Also, external pressures, such as the competition from newer entrants in the business, greater call volumes, rising customer expectations and difficulties of scheduling large numbers of patrols, led AA operations management to conclude that a new system was needed. Traditionally, the AA has been a hierarchical, command and control type of company. In the 1990s this changed, and the management structure was de-layered. AA management thus regard the organisation as much more dynamic. The AA has never been a high-risk organisation. It is all the more surprising, then, that AAHELP was for the most part designed and built in-house, and in a business climate in Europe and elsewhere when outsourcing all or some of the IS/IT function was viewed very favourably. However, as Alistair Cheyne OBE, Director Operations, points out, "We have always been a change company, change comes first you know. There is nothing so constant as change and the speed of change".

1.2.2 Change Management

Change naturally involves risk, and one of the benefits of developing AAHELP has been, according to Alistair Cheyne, that younger, ambitious managers are more prepared to take risks. This is because they have seen that in attempting something that is high risk, as AAHELP was initially perceived to be, there is potential for high returns. The higher the risk, the greater chance for failure however, and in business today, where IS/IT failures are not only spectacular in terms of the large amounts of money spent and lost but also by their sheer numbers, it might have seemed wise for the AA to have decided to continue with its risk-averse business culture. But it decided otherwise. Or, more correctly, certain individuals decided otherwise. Key players in the move to develop AAHELP were Alistair Cheyne (Director Operations), Nigel Brown (Information Systems Manager, AAHELP), Graham Warner (IT General Manager), Tony Liddiard (Information Systems Manager), Nigel Brown (Systems Design, Member Services), Gary Meadows (General Manager, Roadside Operations), Richard Williams (General Manager, Operations Planning and Development) and subsequently Leslie Holt (IT Director, Member Services).

However, it is vital to note that the AAHELP was not 'a project' in the traditional IS project sense. Indeed, this point is, arguably, central to the success of AAHELP; it is part of a wider, ongoing process of change, and as such there was no clear beginning and certainly no definite end point. These key players quickly realised that the Command and Control system, successful though it was at the time, would not be able to meet future business needs. In fact, they had a vision of a networked system that could bypass dispatch, make it automatic and thus improve service (making it faster and more customer-focused), well before the old Command and Control system was developed in the early 1980s.

However, at the time the technology was not yet able to support such a vision. Thus the Command and Control system that was implemented was mainframe-based and had more limited capabilities. "The thrust came from combination of business and IT. There was a recognition in the IT community that the system that we had put in, in the mid 1980s, had got significant limitations" (Leslie Holt). In addition, it was recognised that it was vital to move away from a regionally-organised system to one which was organised nationally.

Another key factor was the role of IT within the organisation. In many organisations IT and the business are separate, with the two rarely interrelating to drive the organisation forward. In the AA both business and IT work closely together. Historically, there were a few IT-led projects aimed at building a bridge between IT and the business function more generally, but they were not successful as they were not 'owned' by any one business within the company. Today, in contrast, IT is well integrated in the organisational structure and reaches deep into each of the businesses. IT and business people work with one another on a daily basis. Whenever business people have a new idea they involve somebody from the IT department. This is to find out how feasible the ideas are, and how best to implement them. The IT group, consisting of about 700 staff, is a central resource that can be 'hired' (and paid for) by different areas of business within the AA. However, each business has its own IT director, who is responsible for systems strategy, business requirements and major projects.

1.3 The aims and objectives of AAHELP

One of the AA's main aims is to remain the number one roadside service in the UK. This could have been achieved by putting more patrols on the road but that would have meant an increase in costs and possibly in membership fees. Staying with the old Command and Control system would have meant expanding the network and increasing the number of operation centres, which would have been a disaster in terms of costs and competitiveness. Without improvements there was a real threat that the number of members would fall. So, the AAHELP system was in part proposed to facilitate improvements in service without increasing costs. AAHELP was targeted at enabling the AA to regain its place as the market leader. This translated into improving the standards of customer service, offering better response times at the roadside, even better fix rate (more cars being repaired at the roadside) and a more personalised service, offering additional benefits and thus increasing customer loyalty. In addition, a reduction in costs was sought, as the objective was to operate at or below market rates. Three main business requirements were identified:

1. **The development of a nationally-based (not regionally-based) system**, where calls from members to the AA would be distributed nationally. This would effectively deal with the problem of a particular operation centre being overstretched, say in the case of very bad weather in one particular geographical region. A national system would enable calls to be spread to a wider pool of call handlers, and to patrols from other regions.

2. **The separation of the functions** of dealing with call handling, and that of deployment. Call handling was a dedicated function dealing with the collection of the member's breakdown details and managed separately from deployment. With AAHELP, deployment is carried out automatically by the computer system itself although, as will be discussed later, not all breakdowns are so simply dealt with.

3. **The provision of a base for new products and services**, such as motor insurance and financial services. These are important if the AA is to continue to expand its business and compete in the competitive marketplace. Having outlined the AAHELP system briefly, what follows is a more detailed look at its development.

1.4 The initial stages of development

As with any software development of any scale the AA looked to see how other organisations managed similar business processes. Vehicle breakdown and recovery is a worldwide business and the AA assumed that there would be several models which would bear scrutiny. However, somewhat surprisingly, no country operated such a national system in the way that the AA envisaged, although there were some small, local, scheduling systems in place in countries such as the US, although with different functionality. Having not found a system that dealt with the scheduling of vehicle breakdown and recovery outside of the UK, some creative thinking was called for.

Tony Liddiard found a company in Sydney which was using a parcel dispatch system that would prove useful in the development of AAHELP. It not only provided a useful model for AAHELP but its success to the parcel company was central to the argument that Alistair Cheyne made to convince the AA Board of Directors.

Getting the agreement of the Board was never an easy task, particularly when large sums of money were involved. It was further complicated by the fact that IT/IS systems were regarded, perhaps, as merely costly administrative support systems and not, as those pioneering the AAHELP system envisaged, a driver for change that would actually enhance the business. Within the organisation itself, the Board of Directors needed even more persuasion than usual; AAHELP was being proposed very shortly after the successful implementation of its predecessor, the expensive Command and Control system. This system was running well, although as with all systems it had its limitations and shortcomings, and it was effectively helping to achieve many business objectives. The proposal of AAHELP was particularly problematic in that it involved a substantial element of risk. No other vehicle breakdown and recovery service in the world had attempted to do what was envisioned for AAHELP. With no similar system to look at, no lessons could be learned from the efforts, and mistakes, of others. Not only this, but developing the system involved leading-edge technology which added further to the size of the risk. If the AAHELP system was to go ahead therefore, it would have to be developed in-house; something that the organisation had not done before and which was, at the time, going somewhat against the trend as outsourcing or buying systems off the shelf was popular. It was also very costly, and difficult to say, precisely, what the benefits would be. For a risk-averse organisation this was going to be problematical. In light of the risk, those championing the development of AAHELP decided that it would be easier to persuade the Board to go ahead and spend the money if the task was divided into several chunks, or phases. If the first phase proved successful, it would follow that it would be easier to persuade the Board to go ahead with further phases. AAHELP was therefore developed phase-by-phase with a business case presented for each phase. Resources were then allocated on the basis of the business case, and for only a six-month period at a time. The phased development had its disadvantages. It added to the total cost of the project, for example the cost of supporting the system during the years that it was being developed. On the other hand, it allowed for a certain degree of flexibility, as the system could be adapted in order to deal with the changes in the organisation more generally and thus be better aligned to the business processes supporting it. In terms of timescale, it took over a year to convince the Board and the different financial teams involved to commit, and there were times when the future of AAHELP was not assured. Indeed, there were those who were not convinced that such a system would work at all. Research and analysis was conducted into the internal skills of the organisation in order to assess the feasibility of developing it in-house, and an external auditor was appointed which, as Alistair Cheyne comments, "led us to the conclusion that we were absolutely right that this was the way to go". Key to its success was recognition that the right key people were already in place, and for all stages of its development. This point cannot be over-emphasised, and indeed is a factor that is constantly referred to by those involved in championing AAHELP.

It was important that the first phase was successful as this would be used to convince the Board to go ahead with the later phases. There was no question in the minds of those championing AAHELP as to which aspect of the business needed to be dealt with first; call handling. The business case stated that the new system would make call handling more efficient, and would ensure a consistency of service, as well as provide additional functionality such as links to customer files. The beginnings of the system started in 1993 with the feasibility stage. After fairly rigorous inspections by key suppliers, it was approved at the end of 1992. The actual design started around May 1992, with the prototype ready by August 1992. The first release into the live environment was ready for April 1994, that is, about fifteen months after its approval. The plan was that each phase should take six months to deliver. That proved overly ambitious and on average each took about eight months. This was in part due to the inevitable additional requirements. The second phase took place in 1995, with the 'final' system being delivered in September 1996. In 1997 the first trial of dynamic re-scheduling took place. The case for automatic scheduling was sound. It was expected to be able to deal with increased calls (for example, during peaks), which in turn would ensure better and more consistent service levels, free dispatchers from low-level, routine dispatching and instead allow them to manage tasks which the computer system could not handle. Although the system can automatically dispatch patrols to routine breakdowns, exceptional cases are handled manually, with little under 20% of the business handled in this way.

One part of the final phase, that is, dynamic re-scheduling, was much more futuristic as it was going to manage the jobs in real time. So, for example, if the initially assigned patrol became delayed the job would be given to another patrol. At this stage a choice had to be made between upgrading the existing solutions and radically re-designing business process. The decision to take a radical new approach to solving the dynamic scheduling problem was taken following thorough analysis of the deployment process and whether it could be automated. Several prototypes were tested before the decision to develop a more radical version was reached, and board approval to proceed was given.

1.5 Functions of the AAHELP system

The nationwide network of centres, which handles all the incoming calls from members who have broken down and need assistance, numbers six million calls a year (around 16,500 a day), and involves some 40,000 incoming and outgoing telephone calls. Over 80% of these calls are dispatched automatically to patrols without any manual intervention once the call handler has completed the call. The remaining 20% require some involvement from deployment staff either to incident-manage the job or change the decision made by the system. The AA currently employs around 800 staff in its emergency call centres and 400 staff in deployment centres, and there are 3,600 patrols out on the roads to assist members who have broken down.

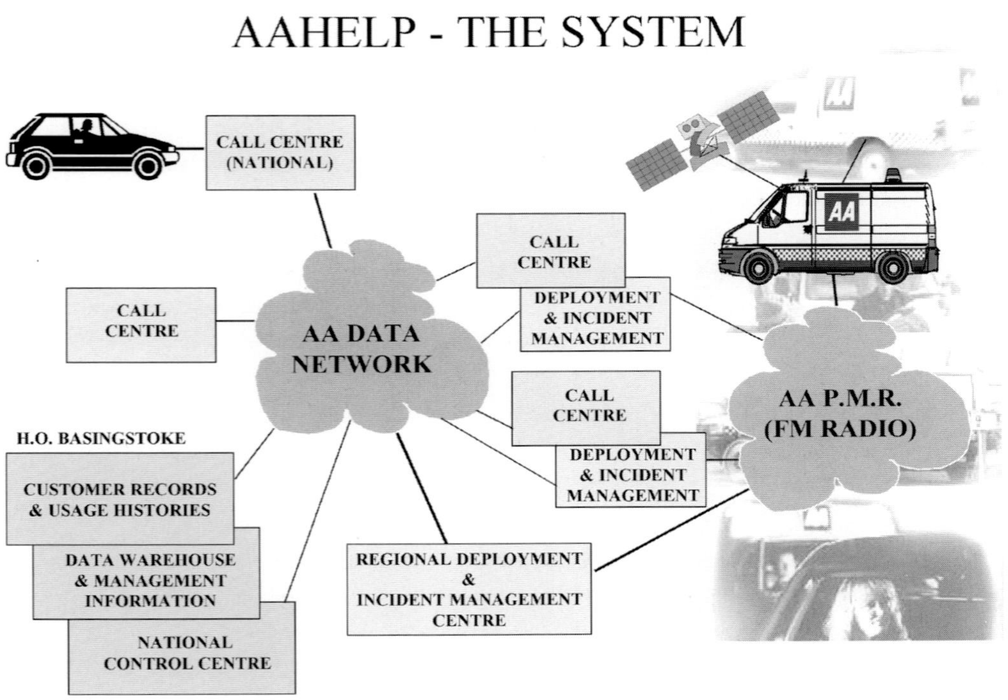

Figure 1 The AA Data Network

A major part of the system is a work-re-scheduling module, which automates the allocation and transmission of breakdown details to patrols. AAHELP was designed as an open system in order to afford maximum flexibility and to serve as a platform for new modules, and it is important to note that it is constantly being revised or added to in order to better support the business. Its four main functions are now described:

1. **A link to a database**. This database, known as the Gazetter, is an electronic map of the UK and also contains locations of useful reference points such as landmarks, and helps the call handler to find the location of the member who has broken down; essential if the patrol is to be sent quickly to the right place! It also allows the call handler to verify that the caller is, in fact, a bona fide member, and what kind of membership the member has. Calls are made to a single national number and allocated automatically to the next available call handler. Each call handler is assigned a personal code, and at the start of each period of work (call handlers work in shifts rather than normal office hours) the input of this code is then used to automatically assign them calls. Calls are therefore allocated on the basis of availability and specialisation.

2. **A diagnostics system**. This prompts call handlers to ask a set of questions about the nature of the breakdown in order to identify the type of problem. The single-source-completion system is highly successful in this regard, and allows the AA to send the appropriately equipped patrol to the member. The AA's competitors are more likely to have the vehicle towed to a garage for repair, and so the AA can only maintain its advantage by sending the right patrol.

3. **Automatic deployment of the patrols**. While the member is still on the telephone, the system automatically makes the decision about which patrol to send, and when. This information can then be given to the member there and then; thus alleviating some of the stress and worry of having broken down. Estimating the time of arrival was somewhat erratic under the old system, and so being able to give the member an accurate time was a major step forward resulting in improved membership satisfaction. Dispatchers can monitor the status of each patrol via the screens on their desks. Each dispatcher has a workstation with dual screens; one displaying text information about a particular job or a summary of all jobs and their status, the other showing the map of the area with patrols and their status. Highlighting a job on one screen will automatically highlight (by flashing) a patrol on the other screen, and vice versa.

4. **Communication between the patrol and the operations centre**. Mobile Data Terminals (MDTs) are installed in the vehicles used by the patrols. Data messages can be exchanged between patrols and the operations centres, with voice being used only in exceptional cases. The patrols are alerted to the breakdown by the display on their screen in their vehicle. The MDT also displays other relevant details, such as the location of the vehicle that has broken down (address and location on the roadmap), the name of the caller and their contact number (so the patrol can call them direct, without having to go back through the call handler), a description of the car, as well as estimated journey and repair time. The patrol inputs a code to accept the job. Once a patrol has made contact with the member who has called for assistance, they must confirm arrival by entering another MDT code. If a repair is completed the breakdown and repair details must be entered.

1.6 The overall management of the AAHELP system

In the middle of the 1980s the AA adopted a project management methodology called PRINCE, which was initially developed for the Civil Service in the UK. PRINCE was adapted and applied to manage AAHELP, and the methodology provided the framework for the involvement of users and their managers, and for change management and risk assessment. Quality was assessed at different stages of the system development. For example, the Project Assurance Team (PAT), which included a mixture of business and IT people, undertook (and still undertakes) quality assurance checking of specifications for new developments before the systems are built. The PAT team is one of the key parts of PRINCE. This is "because it is easy to think you know what the business wants and produce it, and find that it isn't what the business needs", according to Leslie Holt. Internal and external audits were conducted to assess customer satisfaction. Based on this experience the AA developed what it is now called AAPrince, a version tailored to the AA needs. It covers ranges of projects from small to big. Alistair Cheyne is a firm advocate of this approach, and comments that he has seen its power and thus applies AAPrince to not only IT development but to other, non-IT, projects of the business as well.
AAHELP is overseen by a Project Board and supporting teams. At the time of implementation the Project Board, the main steering group for AAHELP, was made up of eight business and three technical representatives; it included four directors from the Member Services Board. The project team included people from different disciplines and backgrounds, and as Richard Williams, General Manager, Operations Planning and Development notes, this had the advantage of "bringing a very diverse blend of skills together". The project team was non-hierarchical. IT people worked together with operational people. Different members of the team had different roles but to some extent everyone was involved in the development. This of course varied, with some people being involved 100% of time, while others 10%. There were a lot

of brief executive meetings. To cover more details, these would then be continued in smaller teams, sometimes outside the workplace in convivial surroundings such as a restaurant. The meetings were attended by operations people from all over the country, and not only helped people to be informed and to communicate ideas but also to bond together. In a sense, the PRINCE methodology was the framework for the management of the task. The work, and organisation, of the people was seen as key to the success of AAHELP, and was referred to time and time again when discussing the success of AAHELP. It is therefore important to make the comment here that although much of the communication was done formally, that is, in scheduled meetings, much of the discussion and decision-making was in fact done informally, that is, in unscheduled meetings both in the workplace and outside of it. Another key point related to this is that these meetings were short, and very frequent. The centrality of teamwork is demonstrated by the comments from Alistair Cheyne, who notes that although there were between 80 and 90 people working on AAHELP, "they all felt as if they had an input into its birth. Some of their ideas and thoughts were in there, therefore their pride was at stake, it was their baby. It wasn't something that was being thrust upon them to develop. If you get involvement right at the beginning you have ownership. And if you have ownership you are a stakeholder... I am not just saying that. It was a showing of us *together*, and problem-solving *together*, and brainstorming *together*. Some of the guys turned out to be tremendous friends, not just colleagues. So you get that loyalty bit." In short, the success of the system was due not only to having the right technology but, more importantly, having the right people.

1.6.1 AAHELP system development: the people

The IT team comprised up to 70 people, each with different capabilities and expertise. Only around 25 had actual programming skills. Some, who perhaps had less experience of designing or programming information systems, had a good understanding of business functions and may also have had particular experience of working on the previous Command and Control system. Although three contractors, with good programming knowledge, were employed at the time, most of the work was done in-house. Although the system was a team effort, there were about five core people who had a vital role in the development of the system and architecture software. The person appointed to oversee the development of AAHELP at the time, together with Tony Liddiard, took a deliberate decision to take the team out of the normal company structure. This separate group was set up and, it was agreed that despite the fact that the AA had centres across the country, this team would work together at one location only. As Tony notes "I do believe that it was a major success to have it set up that way, because by cutting ourselves out of the normal company structure we created a team spirit." Working so closely together enabled a great deal of informal, rather than formal, contact. This meant that a lot of the bureaucracy associated with formal meetings was avoided; people communicated with each other face to face rather than sending emails and producing reports or notes. For example, testers would quickly point out problems to programmers, who would then act upon this immediately. The advantages in terms of time and effort of working in this way are demonstrated in the comment from Tony Liddiard, who notes that "what actually would normally take two weeks, took one afternoon". Similarly, the relationship between Tony and another colleague, Gary Meadows, General Manager Roadside Operations, one of the champions of the project from the business side, was based on informal contacts. They spoke daily, exchanging ideas about the system and discussing problems, and held weekly meetings using a video link, as they were geographically separated by some 200 miles.

During the development of AAHELP seven teams were set up. Numbers in each team are approximate, as this fluctuated over time but gives some idea of the scale of the operation:

1. **The infrastructure team**, which consisted of three to four people, and who dealt exclusively with the infrastructure, everything from the acquisition and installation of hardware down to power supplies and air conditioning.

2. **The design team**. These three people had to produce the detailed design documentation, and their role was overseen by the technical manager.

3. **The build team**, the 20 or so people who were responsible for the actual programming side.

4. **The technical team**, whose three members were responsible for configuration management.

5. **The verification test team**, who conducted technical and system tests. 'White box testing', concerned with how the particular functions and the whole system work, was carried out by the eight people in this group.

6. **The user acceptance team**, which comprised ten people and involved the testing of new developments and end products before they were delivered. This was 'black box' testing, that is, checking what the system did, its outputs and how acceptable it was to the users.

7. **The maintenance team**. The five people who formed this group first came together after the delivery of the initial elements of AAHELP were rolled out. They managed the interface with the users and were their first point of contact.

Overseeing these seven teams was Tony Liddiard. Each of the seven groups had a manager, who reported to Tony, and there were several people who were members of various teams. The user acceptance team had a very important role to play as they tested not only if the system met the specifications but also if it met the expectations of the users, that is, the call handlers and dispatchers. The importance of users to the development of the system is demonstrated by this comment from Tony Liddiard, who says that "You ought to check whether it feels right rather than if it's just built to what we said we would like it to be. Obviously all projects suffer if you build to the specifications... it is rarely the specification that the customer wants at the end of the day, so we are trying to bridge that gap through the user acceptance team". Systems development is thus a continuous dialogue between builders and users, and, as Tony suggests, all did not run smoothly and sequentially as "various parts of the system were built backwards ... the more complicated and important the area, the less likely it was to run to the specification". Thus not all specifications are, in the end, built into the resulting system, as was the case with AAHELP, when on some occasions the specifications were not followed rigorously.

1.7 AAHELP system development: technical specifications

The screens of the call handlers and dispatchers are Compaq PCs running under Windows NT. There are 34 ICL 600 Sparc servers running on a Unix operating system with Ingres databases. The dynamic re-scheduling application runs on dedicated Sun servers. Using open systems architecture means that the equipment and software can be shared and work can be switched between different Centres. The applications are written in Visual Basic and C++. There are 3600 patrols equipped with MDTs (Mobile Data Terminals) and GPS satellite positioning technology.

1.8 AAHELP system development: the software

The majority of the system was developed in-house, although certain components of the re-scheduling algorithm were acquired from the previously mentioned company, Dynamic Transport Management of Melbourne, Australia. Overall, less than half of the re-scheduling software was developed in Australia. The integration of the software, and the design and build of the remainder, was undertaken by the AA's in-house team. Also, surprisingly, although some elements could have been bought in, it was considered faster to write them from scratch than to go through the company approval process. This strategy has proved to be successful, although it was considered a high-risk one at the time. The system was built as a component-based system, using an object oriented approach. General principles and concepts of object oriented design were applied rather than a particular methodology. Different development styles were applied depending upon the business importance of the function. Some areas were prototyped, and they evolved as the project team learned more about the problems. The more traditional applications were built using a traditional, structured approach. This freed more time to devote to the more important and challenging areas. Early prototypes were also used to support the business case in order to illustrate how the system might look and what it would do. Those core to AAHELP were able to exercise a significant degree of freedom in the way they developed the system. Tony Liddiard notes that "we set up our procedures to work as a team, and then we would apply the process, where we felt the processes would gain a result. We applied other techniques where they were necessary to keep it moving. The people that can work in that way generally find it more satisfying", although he cautions that it is important that overall control is effectively managed.

To assist system development activities, an EML case tool was used; this supports various methodologies. It was largely used as a data repository and as a semi-sophisticated drawing tool, and its application was not too formal. Tony Liddiard encouraged people to think about the structure of the system and the logic behind it rather than to argue about the syntax of diagrams. It was seen as important that such a tool should support the system development activities and not obstruct them. Similarly, different approaches were adopted in producing the system documentation. The documentation, its type and level of detail, varies depending on which part of the system it refers to. Some, more traditional, parts are well documented. Others, such as those related to the dispatch application are less so. There is the necessary functional requirements specification, giving the top-level overview, or functional breakdown against the requirements specification together with a compliance statement.

The delivery was organised as a phased rollover. Thus, for example, during the deployment phase one of the call centres and deployment and incident management centres (in Cheadle, Cheshire) was simultaneously running both the old and new systems for a month. In terms of deciding where to trial the system, the choice was made to introduce it in an area with a lower volume of breakdowns, and so Cumbria became a pilot centre. If one part was causing problems, it would have been switched off until those problems were sorted out, and in the meantime, calls could easily be diverted to another centre to be handled and with little loss of service to the member who needed assistance. Once such a trial had been successfully completed, the AAHELP team was then able to go on to the next phase. This gradual, incremental approach to the development of the system meant that although it may have increased the time taken to roll out the system, it had the benefit of working well from the beginning. Indeed, this was central to its success, and the deliberate decision to 'get it right' for the users, from day one, was a key goal. The opinion of those involved with AAHELP was that without the support of the users, the system would not work well, if at all, and that an initially poor system would mean that users would be harder to persuade to switch to using the new system. The old Command and Control system was not only seen as reasonably good but it was also popular. The new system would have to be seen to be delivering great benefit if the users were to switch allegiance. This is particularly important as AAHELP was not merely a system designed to automate what was done manually before, or just a new way of doing what the old system did, but was instead a major change to the way that core activities were carried out by both call handlers, dispatchers and the patrols. Indeed, it not only changed their tasks but also affected their hours of work, responsibilities and patterns of interaction, and thus getting them on board from the beginning was central to the eventual success of the system.

A 'system' is much more than the technology on the desk, and this was something that was very much at the heart of AA management. With this in mind, the system was fairly stable from the very beginning and the (relatively minor) problems that occurred were dealt with promptly. They were not only dealt with quickly but the maintenance team, always on hand, together with the availability and frequent presence of Tony Liddiard, was carefully designed to ensure that, as far as was possible, the users were more than merely recipients of the system.

1.9 AAHELP system development: user involvement

AAHELP "was very much driven by users and it was all based on teamwork between the users and the IT team" notes Richard Williams. Five representatives were chosen by relevant business managers from among the user population and became full-time members of the team. Their job was to undertake verification of the developed software prior to implementation. They also presented their point of view with regard to the system and to explain to the IT team about their work practices. They could consult their colleagues but ultimately it was up to them to present a unified view of their needs. By involving them on full-time basis, and throughout the development of AAHELP, a small number of users were seen to guarantee a consistent view of the business as presented to the IT team. 'Users' is a broad term and involved patrols as well as call handlers and dispatchers. The initiative, or the aims and objectives for AAHELP, came from the business side of the organisation, and many of these, more senior, members of staff were either on the Project Board or in supporting teams. The role of other operational users, that is, the call handlers and dispatchers (rather than managers and directors) was not limited to passive acceptance of the system, they were not merely told about the new system and then given training but were instead consulted throughout the project. Although one of the problems with a representative sample is that there is always the question of whether they are, in fact, representative, their involvement was seen as key to the eventual success of AAHELP. A full-time user manager was responsible for co-ordinating and gathering user requirements, and users were encouraged to make suggestions without taking into account any constraints involving technology. It was user representatives who produced the requirements document. These requirements were not final but were then negotiated with the IT team. The translation of users' requirements was managed through a Joint Application Development (JAD) process involving both users and IT staff, with the final specifications written by the IT team. Designers responded to requirements through compliance statements, specifying what could, or could not, be developed. Any non-compliance with a requirement was referred to a Senior User Committee, who made the decision whether to accept or reject the non-compliance. To some degree the prototypes of the system were used to support communication between the IT team and users, and to help users to visualise the new system, although both those on the management side and users themselves expressed the wish for even greater dialogue. At the later stages of the system development, after the Functional Requirements Specifications (FRS) were finalised, the users could only request certain low-level changes, for example, changes to the look of the screens. They could not, therefore, change what the system did, although it should be noted that key functions performed through screens tended to remain stable. However, it should be remembered that one of the biggest decisions with regard to AAHELP, that is, the de-coupling of the work now done separately by call handlers and dispatchers, was not something initiated by the users but was instead the driving force behind the development of AAHELP, and was instigated by the key players on the IT side of the organisation. There were, then, some higher-level decisions that the users played no part in, and thus it was essential that the major re-structuring of their roles was handled with sensitivity and care.

The attention paid to the involvement of users may in part account for the fact that AAHELP was well received. Although both management and users reported the kind of minor problems that are normal in any system, particularly one of this size and complexity, AAHELP was roundly praised. We accompanied a patrol for a look at how the MDT (Mobile Data Terminal) functioned. Although the patrol concerned had not worked for the AA under the old Command and Control system, he was very enthusiastic indeed about AAHELP. He said that it rarely broke down, and that if it did, this was usually during modifications. However, because everyone relies on the system, the results of any problems can be severe. "When it works right it is a fantastic system, when it crashes it is a nightmare", said the patrol. However, what is good about the system is that "it gets you to the nearest job"; just what the system was designed to make happen. Members are pleased with such a prompt service and their obvious satisfaction with the service was notable. Naturally, their satisfaction might just as well be attributable to the fact that their vehicles were repaired quickly or, just as plausibly, that the particular patrol interviewed was unhesitatingly helpful and polite. However, this is perhaps a little cynical and, if the patrol interviewed was indeed representative, then it is certainly the case that it works well. As a new recruit, and an enthusiastic person generally, the patrol did not feel troubled by working practices that the new system facilitated, for example, having to input codes after each action or being constantly monitored. Although he found hundreds of codes "a bit intimidating at first", he reported that he soon learned the skills needed. Although he had no previous computer-related experience he did not take long to learn how to use in-vehicle Mobile Data Terminal. The importance that the AA places on induction and training is exemplary. In addition to the initial training, the patrol reported that he receives ongoing, off-the-job training and development, which takes the form of five or six days of training a year. The training is on different matters, for example, technical training, or updates on the current system. It is interesting to note that when the system was being developed, the patrols were kept informed of developments, prior and during the release of elements of the system, by the issue of cassette tapes they could play while driving to their next breakdown. However, not all patrols are so impressed with AAHELP and some, particularly older, long-serving patrolmen found the change difficult. This was in part due to the system itself and in part to do with adjusting to the new working practices which resulted from its implementation. However, change is always problematic, and it would be unusual to find 100% agreement from staff about changes to their work, particularly given the far-reaching ones that AAHELP brought about.

The dispatchers interviewed were quite enthusiastic about the system itself, and the new ways of working. One described it as "by far the best". They were also pleased with the way the changeover happened, particularly having such close links with the IT team. However, as with the implementation of any new system, this does not mean that there were no initial problems. The response from call handlers was mixed. On the one hand some were very enthusiastic indeed, and commented that the system was working well and was easy to use. Others had their reservations. They complained that response times were not fast enough, particularly at busy times, although this is addressed by way of frequent hardware upgrades. They also said that crashes affecting parts of the system, together with problems with updates, meant that there was still room for improvement. However, on viewing them at work, the system (on that day at least) appeared to be working fast and well, and the ability of the call handlers, and the system, to send patrols out to members was impressive, to say the least. The job of the call handlers is particularly complicated as they have to deal with members when they are at their least coherent, and when they are in a stressful situation. The call handler must patiently try and get the details from the member, and it is not as easy as it might appear. "And your name, please?" generates "Susan" to which the call handler has to gently prompt "And the *sur*name please?". "What car are you driving?" gets the response "A blue one" and some begin the call with "I don't know if you remember me, but I called last Tuesday", and this to a call centre which handles calls nationally! If this is not difficult enough, there are calls when the member has no idea where they are, and so trying to pinpoint their position in order to send a patrol is made all the more difficult. "Where are you now?" generates "At my brother's house"; one of the easier locations to find! Although the caller does not realise it, the call handler is deftly calling up one screen after another, to see if the member can be prompted to supply more useful information. Such prompting also ensures that the call handler is talking to the right Mr Smith of London driving a Ford Escort (the most common name, place and vehicle in the UK). While the caller is still on the telephone, the patrol has, within minutes (depending on the coherence of the caller!) been sent to their assistance. Overall, then, an IS/IT success, at least from the viewpoint of the users, so attention now turns to where AAHELP goes from here.

1.10 AAHELP system development: the future

In 2000, as a part of a trial, some patrol vehicles will be equipped with a PC that will enable them to carry out automatic diagnostics of faults. Also, the AA is interested in harnessing the potential of telematics. An integrated telematics system in patrol's van would bring together a number of technologies, such as mobile phones with capabilities to transmit data. The aim would be to provide information services such as traffic congestion and route information. Eventually, such systems (perhaps using cellular network positioning) will be hand-held, and not just available in the patrol vehicle. Also, car telematics could support automated call handling. Future developments might see the member's vehicle itself be fitted with sensor equipment that could, for example, alert the AA to a potential, rather than an actual, problem. Such an in-car management system would therefore be able to deliver the information directly to patrols automatically. Thus, in some cases a lot of work would be done by one bit of technology talking to another bit of technology.

As Alistair Cheyne comments, "I think the technology will gradually overtake the need for members to talk to call handlers. Within five years there will be highly automated process within the car, talking to our computer systems and delivering the solution to the patrol. But with some very clever things going on in the background which would give the member reassurance about the process". However, whether members who have broken down, and perhaps are in a stressful situation, would want 'the system', rather than a human being, to deal with them, either at the end of a telephone or via their in-car system is an interesting dilemma, not only for the AA but also for other organisations intending to automate aspects of the business. Indeed, Alistair concedes that some members would prefer to speak to people and that call handling will not be eliminated altogether.

1.11 The benefits of AAHELP to the organisation

This section will look at how success has been measured and judged, and then discuss the benefits in terms of four aspects:

- Cost
- Performance
- Customer focus
- Strategic change

The success of AAHELP has been recognised not only within the organisation itself but also by those unconnected with it. In addition to the BCS Information Systems Management Award in 1999, the AA also won the Millennium Award from the British Design Council and the Institute of Transport Management Award. Before the development of AAHELP, the AA was in danger of losing its number one position as the premier road vehicle recovery service in the UK. Following the success of AAHELP, surveys carried out by *Which?*, as well as those carried out by JD Power, the leading reporters on cars in the UK, confirmed the AA's return to the top. Turning to the measuring of success within the organisation, internal auditors, well known in the industry, anecdotally at least, for being notoriously difficult to satisfy, considered AAHELP a success.

1.11.1 Cost

AAHELP cost £35 million to develop and the return on this investment per year has been calculated at £25 million. The figure includes cost reduction and improved service, taking into account how much it would cost to provide the same level of service, but without AAHELP. With AAHELP the same standard of service could have been maintained with lower costs or, as has been the case, achieving a higher level of service but without an increase in costs. AAHELP has been "vital in re-establishing market leadership with much improved customer satisfaction and business efficiency", comments Alistair Cheyne. Membership decline has been halted and customer satisfaction is at an all time high, as can be seen from figure 2:

	AA	RAC	Green Flag
We're faster	33 mins	40.5 mins	36 mins
		average time to arrive	
	91%	84%	89%
		% of breakdowns attended within 1 hour	
We fix more cars	83%	68%	60%
		roadside fix rate	
We pride ourselves on customer service	91%	78%	none quoted
		calls answered within 15 seconds	

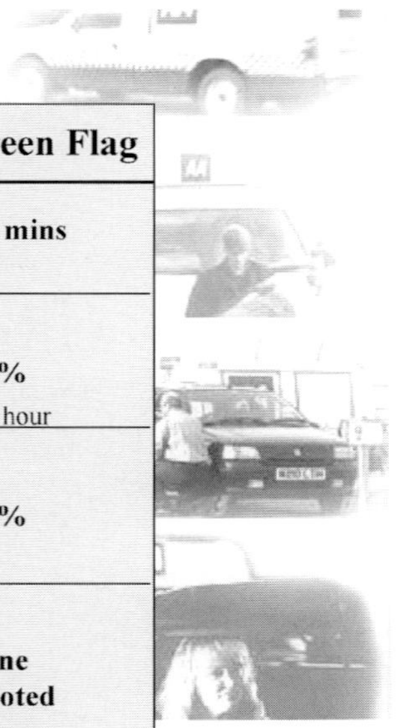

Figure 2 The AA and its competitors

Since the middle of 1993 the AA has measured its members view of the service on a monthly basis. Each month detailed questionnaires are sent to 2% of AA members who have used the service. This is a massive exercise, and involves the collecting of data from 4.5 million breakdowns; one in every 34 breakdowns is sent a questionnaire. The response rate is 46%. The questionnaire seeks members' view on the AA's performance in terms of call handling, speed of response, the quality of service, and the attitude of the patrol. The responses are analysed by an independent organisation (Sample Survey Limited in the UK). From this a monthly MSI (Members Satisfaction Index) is produced.

1.11.2 Performance

Turning to the second of the four aspects of benefits, that is, performance, the implementation of AAHELP has improved this in a number of areas. The speed of response decreased from 47 minutes in 1995 to 35 minutes in 1998, which was better than all of the AA's major competitors. Calls are answered more quickly, and responses are more consistent. The number of vehicles repaired at the roadside (the fix rate) has also improved. These are all benefits that are not only good for the organisation but also can be seen as improving the service for the members.

1.11.3 Customer focus

Since the development of AAHELP, the AA has become even more customer focused, and the benefits in this third area are perhaps less tangible yet equally important. In 1993 the AA set up a series of focus groups with its members. These showed that people not only expected the AA to arrive quickly and to repair the vehicle at the roadside, but also that they expected the AA to deal with consequences of the breakdown, for example, not being able to get to a business appointment, or to pick up children from school on time. In short, they wanted more, and they also expected a personal touch. AAHELP incorporates incident management functionality, which enables the AA to provide a unique solution to every member's particular need. This ability is one of the differentiators between the AA and its competitors. This focus on the interpersonal aspects of interaction with members is evidenced by the change in describing what the call handlers do. Instead of dealing with 'jobs', they now deal with 'members'. A superficial change to some, perhaps, but this reflects a subtle change in the culture of the business, and one which management no doubt hopes will mean a better service to its customers. This change in the business culture also filters through to the dispatchers, where the job is now described in terms of incident handling rather than scheduling of jobs. It is certainly the case that, as over 90% of jobs are being dispatched automatically by the system, dispatchers can spend more time looking after the needs of customers, and also patrols. The diagnostic module assisting call handlers in determining the problem has helped to increase the number of breakdowns that can be completed by one intervention, that is, the assistance of the patrol rather than, for example, the patrol and then the garage agent.

The 'user-friendliness' of the system, flexible work procedures and multi-skilling ensure that other workers can do the job of the call handlers, thus ensuring that calls are answered quickly even on very busy days. Some call handlers have chosen to work from home (telework), and can therefore provide extra cover at busy times.

The work of patrols has become more customer-centred as well. First of all, the areas that they cover reflect demand patterns rather than historically assigned geographic areas known as 'patches'. Also, their working hours reflect time-based demand patterns, thus shifts are no longer of the same length of time. This in turn means that office-based staff and patrols work longer hours in the winter, when their services are more in demand as the weather is worse, and thus work fewer hours in the summer. It is lucky that this coincides with the British preference for taking annual holidays in the summer; the reverse would be more problematic. The way that the AA deals with suppliers has changed as well. In the later stages of AAHELP, the idea of a supply sharing management had been explored, and EDI links have been established with garages. At present about 60% of work going to garage contractors is via EDI links. This speeds up the process and eliminates many routine calls, thus enabling the call handlers to deal with other members.

1.11.4 Strategic change

The last area of benefits is related to strategic change, and it is here that the less-easily measured aspects are to be found. The word 'strategic' is also much used in the literature in describing organisational change and benefits, and yet it is not clear what, precisely, this means. In the case of the AA, strategic change is described in terms of both tangible and intangible aspects. These benefits include:

- The reduction in call centres (from eight to four) and deployment centres (from eight to three).
- The geographical uncoupling of the functions carried out by these two areas of the business.
- The opportunity to telework.
- The way in which suppliers are dealt with.
- Performance management.
- The assigning of work to staff according to customer-driven needs.

Benefits are also described in terms of facilitating multiskilling, improving workflow, allowing for the central coordination of resources and business continuity, enabling an Incident Management service that is tailored to an individual member's needs and last, but not least, improving the morale of employees in the organisation.

1.12 Managing change

The new system required a lot of cultural change in the organisation because it affected in many ways a number of key functions of the business, namely the tasks of the call handlers, the dispatchers and the patrols, and these are now discussed in turn. The call handler's job was (and still is) to answer calls from customers and take down their personal details and those of the breakdown itself. The old Command and Control system was mainframe-based, and there were only two screens. Perhaps it was easier to use because it offered fewer options. AAHELP is very different in that it is Windows-based, and has many in-built functions (like the Gazetteer). On the other hand, with the old system the call handler had to try to assess the problem so the right vehicle could be send to do the job. However the call handler was not a car mechanic and so found assessment difficult. This is now done by the system, which has built-in diagnostic, artificial intelligence capabilities to prompt a number of questions and make decisions about what sort of breakdown it is. New functions were introduced gradually so as to prevent the staff from being overwhelmed by change. Call handlers received general training on how to use Windows by way of a three-hour CBT package, then on AAHELP specifically. According to team managers the changeover to the new system was straightforward. Generally, newer staff accepted the system more easily than older ones. Although not everyone had a chance to state their requirements while the system was being developed, now as a part of the 'ideas in action' initiative, they can put proposals forward to their team leaders, who then pass them on to those in IT. As a result of the new system the work of call handlers can be monitored more easily. Statistics were produced by the old system as well, but now a detailed work breakdown (number of calls answered, the duration of calls, free periods, official breaks taken) are easily obtainable, and at any time. Call handlers do not seem to resent the fact that they are constantly monitored, and at least they are no longer given unrealistic targets for the duration of calls. Thus they do not feel pressurised to deal with customers quickly.

Probably the biggest change in working practices affected the dispatchers. In the past they needed to allocate patrols or garages to every job. It was a difficult job as a number of factors had to be taken into consideration. With the introduction of the new system, the deployment function became less hands-on, no longer requiring 'fire-fighting' skills. Now, as part of their job, the dispatchers have to watch the system, evaluate it, communicate with patrols using the messaging system and, only rarely, dispatching the jobs manually. Some of them found this change difficult. On too many occasions in the early days of AAHELP they attempted to override the system and make scheduling decisions themselves. They needed to be told to let go and put faith in the system. Each dispatcher used to be supported by a service advisor who would, for example, contact a customer in case of a delay. Currently, service advisors are not assigned to dispatchers on an individual basis. Nevertheless, they still provide the interface between the dispatchers and the patrols or the dispatchers, patrols and customers. All service advisors are multi-skilled and move across three sections: incident management, patrol support and liaison with garages.

For the patrols the biggest change was the loss of voice contact with the dispatchers. They no longer had so many reasons to telephone and ask for information and became even more remote. With the patrols out in their vehicles all day, it is a constant challenge to prevent them from feeling remote from the organisation. Some patrols disliked the automatic scheduling of jobs. Some of them, particularly those covering country areas, were used to patrolling particular 'patches'. With the old system some patrols got to know particular dispatchers and they were able to influence the process of job allocation; for example, they could ask to stay in a particular area. Such informal arrangements became impossible with the computer system. In addition, during the same period, but not as a consequence of AAHELP, new working hours were introduced. The changes meant that patrols worked annualised hours depending on the period of the year, month or day. Furthermore, with GPS (the Global Positioning System) the whereabouts of patrols were easily established. patrols were therefore given less choice regarding geographical areas of work, less ability to negotiate jobs with dispatchers and less chance of having unauthorised breaks. On the other hand, the system facilitated improvements in service (through better incident management, more accurate information about patrol arrival time for customers) which has led to more satisfied customers.

The change process appears to have been managed well. As Alistair Cheyne points out, the only way of successfully dealing with change is "by involvement, communication and training", and that the changes associated with AAHELP were managed more successfully than earlier changes in the AA. There was a formal training programme and also informal communication. As part of the informal communication a number of workshops were run, bringing people together, getting their views, and explaining AAHELP and its impact. The system architects spent a lot of time going out on duty with patrols, as well as conducting surgeries for call handlers and telling what to expect. A number of video and audio tapes were produced that covered aspects of AAHELP. The audio tapes were given to patrols to listen to in their vehicles. During the implementation of the final phase at a pilot site, the technical team stayed with the operational people for a month. They assisted the dispatchers at all times, and there was a least one person from the technical team on each shift. The dispatchers came to know them well, and were able to communicate with them easily. Even now they feel at ease to call them and make comments about the system. This, in the eyes of many in the organisation, was a vital factor in the successful acceptance of the system. The dispatchers also expressed the view that they felt that they could better communicate with the IT people as some of the dispatchers were working with the IT team at their place of work rather than being geographically separated from them in the normal course of work. For call handlers, dispatchers and patrols the implementation of the AAHELP system meant major changes, yet the transition from the old to the new was, at worst, uneventful and, at best, welcomed.

1.13 Lessons

Given the problems associated with IT enabled change in organisations it is hoped that the case of AAHELP has the potential to usefully inform others embarking on similar ventures. The case itself reveals many lessons and a number of these are worth highlighting. But rather than list a set of 'critical success factors' which tend to over-simplify things we identify a recurring theme; the importance of key players, and their ability to successfully manage change.

1.13.1 Drivers and champions

Central to the success of AAHELP was that the system was the realisation of a long-standing vision of improving roadside services. It was a vision that did not merely look at what might be possible with the current technology of the time but instead took a much longer view and looked at what might be possible once technology caught up and was able to deliver what the AA wanted. As one of the drivers, Richard Williams notes, "I think we were successful because, first of all, the project was business driven ... not by IT". The system arose from real business needs rather than any fascination with new technologies. AAHELP therefore had the clear backing and commitment from many within the organisation. Any project must have its champions, and at different organisational levels. AAHELP had its business and IT champions in the people described throughout this chapter. Interestingly, and somewhat unusually given the high turnover of staff in IS/IT today, the key players had all been with the company for a very long time, many for 35 years or more. Having project champions who have worked at the company for many years may not be necessary for success but it does help, in that such people know the business side very well and that they often have first-hand experience of other similar tasks. It is also the case that their word may carry more weight, and that they have a commitment to the organisation and thus the long-term success of the project.

It is also important to look at the business culture of the organisation itself, and it is here that it can be seen that the AA was forward-looking, that is, they looked at how things might be done, and not how they had been done in the past. They were prepared to carry their vision through and to be accountable for its implementation. It is always important to have the right people to do the job and to make them accountable. Accountability should lay with a particular person or group of people. For an important project, the more senior the person the better. With AAHELP, although IT people are ultimately responsible for delivering technical solutions, the overall responsibility lies with the business side. Project champions, if the experience of the AA is typical, should come from different quarters of the company. They can then help others to understand the system and try to demonstrate its value to them. At the same time they can act as representatives of the users, making their views known. In the AA, this was a job of user representatives on the project team. As Richard Williams remarks, "I think having champions within the patrol force, and at the operations and call centres was again a critical success factor. Having managers who had been controllers, call handlers, and who understood the jobs of those people and were able to speak on their behalf, and act as their champions, I think is important as well". Although individuals, as champions or drivers, are central to the success of AAHELP, and indeed any other system that the AA or another organisation might implement, people also work together, and this issue is now explored both at the level of the organisation and in terms of the development of the particular IS/IT system.

1.13.2 Teamwork within the organisation more generally

Teamwork, how people work together and relate to each other, is very important. That was recognised by the AA and every effort was taken to build team spirit. The enthusiasm of the 'movers and shakers' of AAHELP could not be contained, and it was clear that they felt very much involved in the project and were proud of its achievements. In a sense it was more than just a job, it was their 'baby'. Regardless of level, people must be given credit when it is due. People on the AA project were motivated and recognised for their achievements. This increased their commitment and enthusiasm. However, Alistair Cheyne believes that perhaps even more effort should be spent recognising the success of the team and boosting their morale. Although that was done a lot internally, perhaps they should have got more external credit for their work. As he explains, "There is no better recognition than senior management of the organisation dive bombing the individual and saying 'thank you'. You can increase their earnings as much as you like, and give extra bonuses, but at the end of the day an individual needs to be recognised. So does the team." Much depends, therefore, on the management taking a careful look at what their staff can do. Directors need to recognise that it is vital that they trust and support their own management. Sometimes organisations tend to down-rate their own management and to put a much higher value on external expertise. However, the expertise and capability may already be within the organisation, as the AAHELP system has clearly demonstrated.

1.13.3 Teamwork at the level of the development itself

Management encouraged the introduction of an informal team structure, and in some circumstances, informal work practices. Linked to this is to bring the team physically together; the AA ensured that the team worked on the same floor. This encouraged co-operation and resulted in faster product development. It also helped to harness people's talents and creativity and to make them feel a part of the team. Encouraging people to take ownership of the system might have prevented many of them leaving the organisation. This is particularly important in IT today, where turnover of staff is high and it is difficult to keep skilled people. Indeed, although the salaries paid at the AA are reasonable, they are not exceptional and many IT staff would have been financially better off by moving to another company. They did not go. This might be attributable, in part, to a strong, supportive organisational structure, although also to the fact that it was an unusual and absorbing piece of developmental work in itself. It must be stressed that users, designers and programmers need to work together. Such co-operation may prevent IT staff from introducing technical solutions just for their own sake. On the other hand, it should also lead to non-technical staff better understanding the capabilities of technologies, and thus not opposing some projects simply because they are unfamiliar with the technology. Ultimately, it should result in a better system. This practice is well accepted in the AA. The application of systems analysis and design methodology helped to structure the process and guide the developers. At the same time, because the methodology was not followed slavishly, it meant that the team could concentrate on problems facing them rather than worry and argue about the details. The flexible approach to development proved to be very successful. It helped to concentrate on aspects that were considered vital to the business, and these are often the functions that are the most difficult to develop. Richard Williams remarks, "I think that the chemistry was extremely good between users and group IT, and personal relationships were very important. And teamwork is very important with this kind of project. It is the people at the end who make a difference, and I think that they had an exceptionally good project executive in Alistair Cheyne being able to bring ... humour and common sense".

1.13.4 User involvement

Although having excellent senior members of staff, including those from IT, is essential, another important lesson to be learned from AAHELP is the need for user involvement and close co-operation between the IT team and users; not just directors and managers but also operational staff. This fact was reiterated time and time again by various members of staff and, as Alistair Cheyne points out "The more people that are involved in the development, the more they own it, the more it is their idea". His view was echoed by Richard Williams, who said that " ... [it is important] to take employees along with you to every level rather than just imposing the system on them. Actually involve them. Because they will always surprise you by making it work much better than the designers themselves thought it would. They can deliver much greater benefits if you involve employees from the outset. So the teamwork doesn't just extend across the IT business side, but also includes teamwork right across every level. Every employee is a stakeholder in the system; the call handlers, the patrols, and the other staff, are stakeholders in the system". However, even a success story is not without its problems. At times it seemed that managers may have put too much pressure upon staff. They tried to implement too quickly, and adopted aggressive implementation strategies, which created some tension in the team. However at no time was there a culture of blame; everyone was made to feel part of a whole, well-integrated, team. There were no big failures as such. However, despite the level of communication and staff involvement, Alistair Cheyne and Gary Meadows expressed the view that the time needed to train dispatchers was underestimated. It was also suggested that it would, in hindsight, have been useful to involve garage contractors during the initial stage as their input would have given them a voice in the design of supply chain management.

1.13.5 Managing the project

Clearly, project management is a vital factor in ensuring a project's success. However, 'project management' is as much about 'people management' as managing the actual product, the system, itself. One aspect of project management is thus ensuring people's commitment, user involvement and their acceptance of the project. The other aspect is managing the outputs, for example by rigorous testing, by having quality assurance procedures in place and by keeping (as far as possible) to deadlines. In the AA, the achievement of these objectives was assisted by the application of the AAPrince methodology. Overall, it seems that there was a right mix of formal project management and informal working practices. This helped to foster a culture of mutual understanding, co-operation, and prevented the culture of blame that is often seen in organisations when things do not go very smoothly and people are not willing to take responsibility for their own mistakes. "Although we had a number of project managers, four or five project managers, throughout the life of the project, we were very disciplined in our approach to project management. I think that was one of the critical success factors", says Richard Williams, adding that "we were very disciplined in assessing the changes required in functionality by the various business directors and getting them to put forward sound business cases for any additions to the applications within AAHELP". Staying focused and keeping to objectives emerge as key points, and this is supported by many in the organisation including Alistair Cheyne, who notes that "It was down to people and focus. We didn't drift from the objectives we set ourselves. We set them out very clearly as to what we wanted to do, and we kept the focus on that". Although the team had to accommodate extra requirements, they only accepted them if they could do it after a particular phase which had already started, and would not do so unless it had real commercial value.

It was suggested by some in the organisation that perhaps the developments that were outside the scope of the original proposal should have been more firmly resisted. This is not easy of course, and the balance must be achieved between what is best for the new system and what is best for the organisation more generally. This again emphasises the importance of having the right senior people championing the system; as the experience of the AA demonstrates so clearly, it is these people who have the clear business overview, and the vision, to manage the task itself. However, a new system of the size and complexity of AAHELP is as much, if not more, about managing change itself.

1.13.6 Managing change

Central to the success of any new system, whether an IS/IT one or otherwise, is the management of people's expectations. This was a vital ingredient in the success of AAHELP, as those managing the far-reaching changes were aware of the impact of them and sought to carefully manage them. AAHELP meant major changes to the way that call handlers, dispatchers and patrols, that is, those handling key aspects of the business, carried out their daily tasks. Ensuring their acceptance of the new system was essential, and although the system could have been completed earlier in terms of making the technology work, a longer, slower route was taken as this was felt to better deal with the human aspects involved in systems development. Those involved in the management of AAHELP therefore organised a number of meetings, or surgeries, with staff explaining the system and how it may affect their work. The technical staff took part in the surgeries, and this enabled the non-technical people to ask more specific questions. Whether by accident or design, it also forged a closer relationship between the operations staff (dispatchers in the main) and the technical team. Indeed, Gary Meadows feels that the level of support from the technical staff, together with the strong culture of co-operation in the organisation more generally, were probably the biggest factors in ensuring a smooth changeover process.

However, it is important when managing people's expectations that hopes are not dashed. With this in mind, the champions, or drivers of the system were, in public, cautious when estimating the system's benefits. Privately, they were much more optimistic, and with justification; the system surpassed their expectations and continues to deliver benefits that were not realised either before or during its development. Another factor is clearly the system itself, that is, its stability. However, this was not merely by accident but was carefully managed. The reason behind this decision was sensible, though not often followed in IS/IT development. If people are going to buy into the system, and at the same time radically alter their working patterns, first impressions count.

With this in mind, it was therefore vital that the first time that the call handlers, dispatchers or patrols used the system it worked. Simple enough in theory, but, as countless failures in IS/IT development have shown, clearly not so easy to do in practice. So, when those using the system used it for the first time, they were won over. This is not to say that it was perfect, or that there were not minor problems that needed to be ironed out; no one would claim this, naturally. However, those who used the system immediately saw the benefits that the new system would deliver; they were on board already. This in part explained the decision to have a staggered roll-over, as the new system was introduced gradually and the old one was kept running for a month as a backup; just in case. This safety net is another vital aspect in managing change; most people like to cling on to the familiar before embracing the new.

In the end, all systems development, or indeed any change, is about the management of risk. Richard Williams speaks for many in the organisation when he says that one of the factors in the success of AAHELP was "being prepared to take measured risks and having confidence in employees at all levels". Although not being afraid to take some risks can reap its rewards for an organisation, it goes without saying that there is a price to be paid if the risk taken does not deliver what was expected. Perhaps 'measured' risk is a key word. Thus, although the AA took considerable risks in going ahead with the AAHELP in the first place, and particularly in developing the dynamic re-scheduling module, the risks were calculated and a number of measures were introduced to lower them. Those measures included having phased implementation, producing a business case for each phase, continuous evaluation of the system (AAHELP was formally evaluated every six months, now it is done annually), and external assessment.

However, rather than having comprehensive documentation, which is what these are for the most part, success or failure of an IS/IT system, particularly one as complex as AAHELP, is dependent on the people managing it. So, with inappropriate people presenting the business case or doing the evaluation for example, it is not difficult to see that the resulting system will not work, or will not work as well as it might. Champions, that is, successful leaders and managers of change, use these formal tools to aid them, but the tools in themselves cannot make for a successful system. And identifying the right people for the right task, and at the right time, is a challenge for all organisations.

In short, the success of AAHELP is, as they themselves say, that the AA had the right people. Unfortunately, the 'right people' in one organisation, or on one project, might equally be the 'wrong' ones in another organisation or context. This is an enduring dilemma, and for some, who like the world to be neatly and tidily explained, a worry. For others, it is one of the exciting challenges of IS/IT management in that every project, every person, every organisation, not to mention the context and the culture in which these operate, is unique. In this view there are, then, no 'right people' per se, only the right people for the right task in a particular context. And, as the experience of the AA demonstrates, they had the right people, doing the right things, in the right place, and at the right time!

Chapter 2

Halifax Share Dealing

2.1 Introduction: Building Societies

The first building society was founded as early as 1775 in response to the growing need of individuals to finance the purchase of property, a business that the banks of the time were not particularly interested in supporting. The Halifax was established in 1853 in the town of its name which had reaped the benefits of the industrial revolution and where the skilled and growing white collar population wanted to own their own homes (www.halifax.plc.com). The building societies were established to help finance such purchases by providing a means for people to borrow money. They were sometimes supported or even established by the owners of the mills and the factories as a way of providing for the needs of their workers. The building societies continued to expand and prosper and in the early nineteenth century they also became savings institutions, providing interest to those who wanted to save but not necessarily buy a house. In the early days there were some spectacular building society collapses resulting in regulation and legislation, with the first Building Society Act in 1874 restricting societies to house financing and related borrowing and lending activities. In terms of ownership building societies were typically owned by, and run on behalf of, the people with loans and savings with the society, rather than by equity shareholders.

However, it was the first half of the twentieth century, particularly the inter-war years, that was the 'golden age' of the building society movement with not only an expansion in the number of societies but importantly a great expansion in the number of branches. The Halifax was no exception, indeed it was at the forefront of this growth and with a merger it became the largest building society in the world. In this period the number of customers and the assets of the societies grew substantially on the back of the housing boom. It is estimated that in the inter-war period 4 million houses were built and that of these around 3 million "were very largely financed by the building societies" [see ref. 1 at end of chapter]. One of the factors that fuelled this growth was the high level of owner-occupation in the UK, substantially higher than most other countries. This was a social feature that was politically encouraged and the building societies dominated the financing of these purchases, with the banks still relatively small and disinterested players in this market. By the mid 1980s around 60% of houses were owner-occupied with a relatively small rented sector.

Around this time the banks became more interested in the personal customer rather than just the business and commercial markets and with a certain amount of financial deregulation they began to sell mortgages aggressively. As a result their share of the market rose quickly, from 8% in 1980 to 26% in 1982 [1]. The response of the building societies was twofold. Firstly they cried 'foul' and tried to persuade the government to let them compete on the same basis as the banks and that the restrictions placed on building societies were unfair. Second it was calculated that the way to best compete was to grow in size and develop a larger market share, usually by acquisitions or mergers. In this respect the Halifax was no different, and despite the fact that they were already the largest building society with the largest number of mortgages they wanted also to be effectively the largest retail bank as well. Their mission was to be 'the biggest and best personal finance business in the UK' and so they actively began investigating the possibility of a merger with another major society.

With the Building Societies Act of 1986 the government did indeed free the building societies from some of the restrictions relating to their housing origins and enabled them to undertake a wider range of financial services, such as personal loans, credit cards, estate agency, conveyancing, etc. Significantly it also allowed building societies to convert from mutual status (owned by their members) to public limited companies (plc) with shareholders owning the equity, if they wished. The legislation reduced the advantage that banks were perceived to have but it was still felt by many that in order to compete on an equal footing they would eventually have to take advantage of this option and convert to plc status, or 'demutualise' as it became known. The Halifax concluded that although the 1986 Act allowed building societies a wider range of activities it was still somewhat restrictive.

For example, it required building societies to have 75% of assets made up of loans fully secured on residential property and that at least 50% of funds should be raised from members. Halifax felt they needed access to a wider range of funding sources, such as international equity and debt capital and wholesale funding markets, to enable them to develop new initiatives and diversity into new markets. As a result it was decided that conversion would provide the necessary flexibility for the future.

Of course even if the board wishes to convert the rules required that the society members must vote in favour. Whilst there has been opposition to conversion the fact that it usually results in members receiving free or 'windfall' shares in the new plc company has meant that the vote tends to have large majorities in favour. The Halifax was no exception, with around 72% of eligible members voting, of which 97% were in favour.

2.2 Merger with Leeds

A number of merger possibilities presented themselves to the Halifax but the one that seemed to have most potential was the Leeds Permanent, the fifth largest building society in the country. One factor that may have contributed was that the Halifax Chief Executive, Mike Blackburn, had previously been Chief Executive of the Leeds. After a prolonged period of negotiation it became clear that the Leeds would only agree to a merger if it were to be associated with conversion. According to Pugh (1998) "The Leeds directors wanted a merger, indeed were probably more keen on it than the Halifax directors, but they knew that they could not present the deal to their members without a substantial reward". Conversion to a plc would provide that reward. The Halifax had been toying with the potential benefits of conversion for a number of years which had culminated in a 1988 decision to remain mutual, although it had been a close run thing. Indeed the Report and Accounts of 1994 stated that the Halifax saw its future as mutual and stated that it was healthy not having shareholders to whom dividends had to be paid.

However, the Halifax board decided that the benefits of raising capital, that conversion provided, and the benefits of merging with the Leeds would force their hands. So in November 1994 the Halifax agreed to the merger with the intention of conversion, and all members of the Leeds were treated as if they were members of the Halifax becoming entitled to free shares on conversion. It was possible that the merger would be referred to the Monopolies and Mergers Commission, which might have delayed or vetoed it. In the event it was not referred and the merger went ahead, after the members of both societies voted in favour, on 1st August 1995. The merged organisation had 20 million customers, 20% of the mortgage market and assets of £116 billion [1]. A truly prodigious size.

The effective establishment of a merger is always one of the most difficult elements, and in this case around 28,000 people in 1,800 locations were effected and the process involved the integration and rationalisation of staff, the branches, the financial products and the computer systems from both societies, as well as fulfilling all the regulatory requirements. There were distinctly different cultures in existence and the Halifax was seen as rather regimented, with strong central control, highly procedural, status conscious, and grade driven, with the Leeds as somewhat freer and with a more enabling, innovative, culture. Making it work at all levels particularly on the ground, was a real challenge and turning it into one organisation that speaks with one voice and gets the best of each part needed detail planning if it was to be achieved within eight months. The approach devised was to hold the Halifax in good stead for subsequent activities as we shall see. Controlling overall strategy was a Chairman's Committee consisting of the chairmen, vice-chairmen and executives from both societies. Then there was a Programme Steering Group for the merger and all detailed planning was handled by a Programme Office staffed by people seconded from both societies and John Miller was appointed to direct this Office. Miller had been Director of IT at the Leeds, prior to the merger and before that he was Director of Operations at Orange, the mobile phone company. As will be seen he plays a key role in driving and developing the Halifax Share Dealing Service. The merger itself was successfully achieved but all the work involved was just a preliminary to the next task which was conversion to public limited company status.

2.3 Conversion

The day set for conversion was June 2nd 1997, known as 'Vesting Day' or V day. The period allowed for preparation was just over two years, this was partly due to legal reasons, partly to do with the fact that members holding accounts for two years would get shares, but mainly because that was the length of time it was calculated to take to make the necessary arrangements. The scale of the conversion task was again enormous, possibly even more daunting than the merger. The budget for conversion was set at £150 million, which represented about £20 per member who became a shareholder. The merger process was very challenging due to the large volumes and the importance of meeting the deadline. There was no leeway. If one element was not ready the conversion would fail. It was very high risk, very public, and failure would have had a profound effect on the Halifax, even bringing into question its viability.

Roger Boyes, Finance Director, commented that conversion was "highly complex... and a huge constitutional problem. You have two principal regulators to deal with, the Building Societies Commission and of course the Bank of England who will grant the banking licence. So the whole of the regulatory process, not just from a legal and accounting side, but from a logistics side as well, was monumental'.

2.4 Cleaning up the customer files

The range of activities to be undertaken was enormous but probably the single largest was the cleaning up of the membership registers of the two societies, which was itself described as 'truly a mammoth task'. The existing files were obviously separate for each society and needed to be merged, however, the biggest problem was that the records were account based rather than member based. The files had grown up over time with people opening accounts and details held about them as customers for that particular account. No accurate view of customers, independent of their accounts, was available. The conversion required such a record, as a customer (member) of either society was only allowed one vote, and one share allocation, irrespective of how many accounts they held. This meant that the Halifax had to trawl through all its accounts creating an accurate members register with up to date details of names, addresses, ages, etc. One of the problems was that the details held about customers in relation to each of their accounts frequently differed. Accounts opened by the same person at different times might have different names (married women in particular), different addresses, different ages, etc. and yet it was the same person. They all needed to be checked and cross checked, making sure that no multiples slipped through and no eligible member missed out. This had to be done for both societies and then the membership merged, although this did not end the problem because members of both societies were only to get a single share allocation right. Further, one account only entitled one person to share rights, even though the account might be held in multiple names. In such cases the first named account holder was deemed to have the rights. As can be imagined this caused much resentment and some bad publicity although these were rules specified in the Building Society Act and not decisions made by Halifax.

The clean-up of the members register had to be as accurate as possible, because the rules and regulations stated that the whole conversion could be challenged if the member registers were not accurate. The number of 'account relationships' that had to be checked was over 32 million. Some intelligent computer matching software was used to do the checking and it was able to deal with the bulk of the total but still some 2.8 million records had to be checked by hand. Frequently problems had to be sent to the branches so that they could investigate the details and as a last resort contact the member for clarification. The register also had to be completely up to date and this was an ongoing process as over 1,000 members die each week! The whole task required 350 people centrally plus around another 1,000 in the branches.

Boyes posed the question, "How are we actually going to manage this lot? We had learned some very, very good techniques from the merger. We were all persuaded that programme management, where you have an over-arching programme that is broken down into logical blocks of work and projects within those logical blocks, charters we call them, was the way to go forward again. So we planned the approach to conversion along the same lines with an over-arching board committee, the Conversion Committee, meeting monthly. Then we had the programme directors who were Mike Blackburn leading the charge with his three executives, John Miller, Mike Ellis and me who were directly responsible, meeting weekly. We carved up the task into blocks of work, with Mike Blackburn co-ordinating. Then each of us sub-divided our blocks into individual projects and each one was written up completely and planned in meticulous detail" (Pugh, 1998).

The result was the identification of 20.3 million customers (individuals holding accounts of any kind), 14 million members (those who were over 18 and held investing or borrowing accounts), and 7.6 million people eligible for shares (those who had certain amounts in their account on particular dates over a two year period). In total this meant some 2.5 billion Halifax shares were issued.

2.5 Share Dealing – the decision

The part of conversion which was particularly challenging and risky was that of share issue and dealing. Shares would be allocated to approximately 8 million individuals and it was calculated that about 2 million would sell immediately on the first day, as members cashed in on their windfalls. Halifax decided to set up their own execution only share dealing service for trading in their own shares, with the ability to handle trading in all shares at some future point. An execution only service provides just the ability to buy and sell shares on the instructions of customers, no advice or recommendations are given. Setting up such a service was a positive forward thinking move but might equally have been viewed as imprudent or inadvisable in the short-term. Why would the Halifax saddle itself with an extra, extremely challenging, undertaking in the middle of the biggest conversion in history? Further, share dealing was not a business in which they had experience, and that business could, in theory, be undertaken by existing city institutions, albeit at a large cost, as had been done in other building society conversions.

John Miller, the then Director of Business Strategy and Operations, remembers that decision well. The sheer size of the operation dwarfed the previous experience of the city institutions. Even in the US the largest similar share issue was only to 2 million investors. He says "We had twenty one million members, and they are holding thirty two million products, and the share distribution is absolutely critical. Our advisors said the traditional institutions could work to 99% accuracy, 99% is still two Wembley Stadiums worth of member problems, which was too much... and the way they were going to do it basically would have brought the Stock Exchange to its knees. So like it or not, and despite the best endeavours of the professionals... we came to the conclusion that we had to do it ourselves... We gave everyone the opportunity to offer solutions but nobody really did, at least to our satisfaction. What they were recommending was the traditional way, i.e. dealing with the share issue as a paper based system. So it was back to us, we had to do it".

"It was a very difficult decision because we had to convince the board, and everything was against us, I mean all the classic things. You go down the check list: have you got experience in this area, no; is it big bang from day one, yes; can we give it time, no. So all of the classic things that you are not supposed to do, all were against us."

"The Board was eventually persuaded by pointing out to them that if they went with the recommended option they would have these two Wembley Stadiums of dissatisfied people to deal with, all writing to Watchdog. Not only that but you would need all the trestle tables in Oxfordshire and probably have to hire the National Exhibition Centre to deal with all the paper. I mean it was ludicrous, the more you went through all the practicalities, the more ludicrous it became". The reference to the number of 'Wembley Stadiums' worth of upset customers became something of recurring theme in the Halifax as a result of some of the senior management attending the cup final that year. Looking around the packed stadium was a very visual image of the numbers of customers with problems that an accuracy rate of 99% would provide!

Miller says that "sooner or later sense prevailed, and they (the Board) came along to our way of thinking. And then all of a sudden a rabbit comes out of the hat, that there is another way of doing it... Not only that but it was nine million pounds cheaper, I suppose that had a little bit to do with it!".

Thus the decision was made to undertake the handling of the share issue themselves. Miller may have been right that there was no viable alternative but the challenge was nevertheless daunting. Halifax needed to interact with the Stock Exchange, find a registrar, a receiving bank, liaise with the Bank of England, deal with the regulatory bodies, be deemed 'fit and proper' as individuals, and become a bank, apart from developing a share issue and dealing system.

2.6 Share Dealing – the Nominee Account

The 'rabbit out of the hat' that Miller mentions was the potential use of a nominee account. This meant that it might not be necessary to provide every one of the 8 million qualifying individuals with a share certificate. The ridiculous thing about everyone being issued with a share certificate was that it was estimated that around 2 million members would immediately sell their shares. The paperwork connected with the issue and trading of share certificates was extremely large and costly, particularly when they are sold on immediately. The use of the nominee account could reduce this overhead substantially. A Nominee company is a type of trust company created for the purpose of holding investments on behalf of investors. The individual's name does not appear on the share register, the shares are registered in the name of the nominee company, which has legal title of the investments, although the individual remains the beneficial owner. Communications and dividends are not sent to the individual by the company in which the shares are held but they are sent to the nominee company [2]. Nominee accounts require much less paperwork because dealings are handled electronically, and dealings can occur without waiting for the issue of a share certificate from the company registrar. Of course it was not really a 'rabbit out of a hat' in the sense of a surprise revelation as the concept had been actively researched over many months, including trips by Halifax managers to investigate similar systems in the US. Although his could only be contemplated in the UK if the Stock Exchange could handle settlement electronically but fortuitously they were planning to do just that with the CREST system.

CREST is a computerised system for equity settlement and it meant that shares could be held in electronic form rather than on paper, bringing the Stock Exchange in line with other international markets, and importantly it meant that the nominee holdings could be dematerialised and held electronically. CREST was to be introduced in 1996, which meant that it should be in place for conversion day.

However, although the nominee account meant that they did not have to undertake the bureaucracy of share certificates, it was risky because there were concerns about whether CREST would be ready and whether it would be able to handle the millions of transactions that the conversion would generate. The Stock Exchange did not have a glowing track record with its IT systems and the earlier Taurus System had been a well publicised IT disaster. Although in the end CREST, despite 'lots of teething trouble', was up and running properly by vesting day.

The example of the Abbey National was also constantly in the back of peoples' minds. The Abbey had floated some years earlier and it had been a 'bit of a nightmare'. Of the 4.3 million eligible members who were supposed to receive share certificates 530,000 of them had gone missing, some bizarrely ending up in skips, resulting in customer dissatisfaction, bad publicity, expense and damage to the company. The Halifax had considerably more eligible members and the spectre of these kind of problems helped the Halifax to reject the system used by the Abbey and turn towards the nominee system.

There were also other, more minor, perceived benefits such as the fact that a share register is essentially an open book which anybody can access, whereas the details of a nominee register are not, and this can lead to promotional opportunities. All these benefits combined to provide just what the Halifax wanted and so they decided to go for a 'nominee system'. This meant that the floatation was not just possible but manageable, provided that most of the shareholders opted for the nominee account. It was to be their choice. Halifax attempted to persuade people to opt for the nominee account by providing them with almost all the rights of certificated shareholders, including the annual report and a vote at the annual general meeting. They also established the Halifax Shareholder Account designed to make life easy for the customer and as a secure way for them to hold shares. They were also to be allowed to buy and sell shares via the Halifax Share Dealing Service, without having to keep, and possibly lose, a share certificate. It made 'the holding of shares as easy to manage as having a savings account'. The details of the Shareholder Account, i.e. the customer holding and any sales or purchases, were sent out as a statement on a regular basis, just like the other accounts that the customer was familiar with. The Account was also to be free for at least 3 years and for ten days after conversion trading was also to be free. As it turned out nearly 80% of people opted for the nominee account reducing the number of share certificates required to be produced and handled by about 6.5 million. Halifax also set up a single company PEP (Personal Equity Plan) that provided a tax-free environment for the holding of Halifax shares.

2.7 Communication with members and eligibility for shares

Meanwhile the conversion work was continuing and the volume of communication to members was vast. Most of it determined by the requirements of the regulator but some by the Halifax's desire to keep people informed of what was going on. In total over 65 million conversion related packages were sent out to members. The largest of which was the Transfer Document, posted in January 1997. This contained all the information deemed relevant for members to make a decision on conversion and it went through 15 drafts with the regulator before it was approved. According to Graham Johnston, Assistant General Manager, Corporate Finance, it was "draft, draft, draft, check, check, check – boring and tedious it may have been but the fear of failure concentrated our minds". The Transfer Document ran to 166 pages, and the total mailing used some 5,000 tonnes of paper which was calculated to have required 60% of the UKs total printing capacity (Pugh, 1998, p204). Although all the paper came from renewable sources the Halifax decided to pay for the additional planting of 30,000 trees to offset some of the environmental impact. The Royal Mail was also put under considerable pressure by the Halifax communicating with their members. The Transfer Document needed 12,000 Royal Mail 'cages' but unfortunately they discovered that they only had 5,000!

One particular mailing in November 1996 caused the telephone helpline to stagger and resulted in a great deal of bad feeling. This was the letter where people learned whether they would be eligible or not for the free shares. There were various rules that had to be satisfied. People had to have £100 or more in their accounts on three particular dates over a period of just over two years. There was a fixed number of shares that would be received and then there was a 'variable distribution' which added more shares for those with over £1,000 in their accounts. Accounts in joint names could only have one share allocation and the allocation went to the first named. Those that did not qualify were outraged. Women particularly were affected as they were often second named on joint accounts with their husbands, but also the disabled and the blind who sometimes had other people as first names on their accounts. Children, aged below 18, were also ineligible for shares but were allocated a cash distribution of 9.4% of their account balance.

A large response was anticipated and the helpline was set up to operate 24 hours a day to automatically handle the most common questions using an IVR (interactive voice response) system. 250 operators were then available to handle specific queries and a further 140 to deal with detailed complex queries. On one day nearly 100,000 calls were received with 300,000 in the week. Queues inevitably built up and exacerbated the frustrations. The press were contacted by irate members and some newspapers campaigned on members behalf, castigating the Halifax for their perceived inadequacies. It was a bad time to be a Halifax helpline or branch operator trying to explain why someone was not going to qualify for windfall shares when they thought they should. Additionally over this period the backlog of unanswered letters reached 50,000 despite 15,000 response letters a week being dispatched. More resources and staff were allocated and eventually the backlog was cleared and the uproar declined but nevertheless it was an important lesson for the Halifax and they were determined that it should not happen again.

2.8 Halifax Share Dealing Limited (HSDL)

Having made the decision to go for a share dealing service themselves Halifax had to put all the parts into place to make sure it happened. They established a separate entity, Halifax Share Dealing Limited (HSDL), based in Leeds. A number of people were appointed internally to the new company including Rick Girling who became IT project manager for the share dealing service (now Business Systems Manager of HSDL). One of the key appointments was the Managing Director of HSDL, as Miller says "one of the things that you need in order not to be seen as a circus, and to be credited with the appropriate regulatory sign off, is an experienced person from the industry as the leader of the Business Unit". The Halifax did not have that kind of person in-house so they appointed Sue Concannon from Sharelink. Sharelink were an innovative organisation that had developed an execution only telephone based share dealing service. Miller says "Sue's presence was absolutely essential to implement the final acceptance, and for us to get into the full share dealing service. She also knew how to run a share dealing business, that was her main value added". Unfortunately she was not in position until January 1997, rather later in the day than would have been liked. "Ideally she could have been with us a few months earlier... on the basis that we were breaking a lot of new ground, and doing things totally differently but it might have been at the expense of making the initial project more complex".

2.9 Share dealing objectives

The objectives of the share dealing service were to have a service that the members would find very simple to use and understand. The large majority of the people who were to be allocated shares were not experienced in share dealing and had not owned shares before. They were obtaining their shares by accident and had probably never anticipated being shareholders. Thus they were not the traditional kind of person who deals in stocks and shares and understands the concepts and the terminology. The whole idea can be very intimidating. Thus the design brief was that it should be simple for the customer. As Miller says "How do you explain to Mrs Wrigglesworth, of 4 Railway Cuttings, how the Stock Exchange works, there's no chance. So you have to make it very simple and easy". All the confusing terminology, all the processes and procedures, how to buy and sell shares, had to be explained simply and accurately. Additionally they did not want members to be put off by the cost, particularly in the first instance. Buying and selling, for those who opted for the nominee system, was to be free for ten days, after which a competitive 0.5% commission was charged. A secondary objective was to keep the issues concerned with share dealing away from the branches. This was partly for regulatory reasons but also the pressure on the branches of the conversion activity was heavy, as has been seen in connection with the members register, and for them to have a large scale workload related to share dealing would have been problematic.

The pressure on the branches of the conversion activity was heavy, as has been seen in connection with the members register, but for them to have a large scale workload related to share dealing would have been problematic. They needed to focus on running the traditional business, i.e. dealing with mortgages and savings. So share dealing was designed to be post and telephone call centre based, rather than branch based. It also emphasised the need for ease of understanding because it was known that if anything was not clear to the customer, their immediate response would be to go into their branch and ask questions. This happened of course to some extent but the objective was to minimise it. Miller reflects that "I suppose what came across fairly quickly was that what we were doing here was beyond the experience level of branch staff as well. So not only were you supporting customers but you were supporting the whole of the branch operation. It emphasised the need for training as well".

The longer term objectives concerned the capability for further development and it was recognised early on that it would be possible to make share dealing and related activities a new, revenue generating, business for the Group. The design would be such that although it was initially just Halifax share dealing the ability to offer an all share dealing service should be included.

2.10 The HSDL task

Concannon states that the tasks of HSDL "involved all the systems and software development that was necessary to support these processes. But also establishing the company, recruiting all the staff, designing the process... getting the whole thing regulated and the right documentation for the customers, and seeing that all the way through to the dealing period". In particular, "the shares were going to be distributed to customers and then we had to deal with those who wanted to sell, how they could sell them, and how those shares were going to be passed onto the institutional investors who wanted to buy them". The role of the financial institutions was important as although they would not receive any shares initially they would certainly want to buy immediately they became available, in order to keep their portfolios balanced. This process had to be managed carefully as the potential for volatility in the market was large. Concannon says that "this was one of the difficult things, working out how many people were likely to want to sell and balancing that with the demand from institutional buyers who were desperate to get their hands on Halifax stock. Conversion would take us straight into the Footsie (FTSE 100 – the Financial Times Stock Exchange index of 100 top companies), or very shortly after… and so the institutions needed to have Halifax in their portfolios".

Knowing how many members were likely to want to sell immediately and balancing the demand of the institutions was a key consideration for the Halifax. Concannon says that "Our early research showed quite a low level of selling, but as it got closer and closer to the date then the research got a little more accurate. But certainly the 23% that sold was towards the high end, of the estimate. And I remember we were all completely shocked when the Alliance and Leicester (which demutualised shortly before the Halifax on 21st April 1997) got 27% of their members selling straight away". The Alliance and Leicester also held another lesson which was that their members who sold through the pre-market auction to the institutions could have got a much better price if they had waited and sold in the market on the first day. The Halifax did not want a repetition of this.

In the end they chose to sell to institutions via a competitive real-price blind auction held on the Friday before conversion, supervised by the regulator. Essentially shares were sold to institutions that offered to pay the best price and members received the weighted average of the bids. The shares available to the institutions to buy were those of members indicating, about two weeks before conversion, that they wanted to sell in this way. Those that indicated they did not want to sell could wait for the stock market to open on vesting day.

2.11 Re-thinking the share dealing process

Another example of the way that Halifax was thinking differently to the traditional dealing approach was in relation to the sale (or buying) price in telephone dealing. Traditionally the industry worked by quoting the customer a price and then the customer deciding whether to sell or not. If they decided to sell the price they actually receive is not the quoted price but whatever price is current when the transaction is actually processed, which might be some time later and might be somewhat different. Usually the price difference is only a few pence but nevertheless it is different, occasionally however the difference is significant. The Halifax felt that this difference would be difficult to explain to their customers who had expectations that prices quoted were fixed, as in their other transactions with the Halifax. Also they felt it would cause bad feeling, disputes and require administrative attention. Not only that but as Miller says, "we don't want to explain to our customers how the Stock Exchange works… people want to know the time not how the clock works!".

So they asked if the price quoted could be guaranteed to be the price actually obtained. Miller recalls that this was originally met with scepticism and a degree of concern. Were the customers of HSDL going to be sophisticated enough to understand the concept of real-time prices? Would the price feeds be reliable enough? Could 'best execution' (a regulatory requirement) be guaranteed in such circumstances?

Although some share dealing businesses were already offering real-time trading with price confirmation, the volumes and automated nature of the HSDL setup were very different. Moreover, it was felt that the fact that HSDL's customers were less experienced with stockbroking transactions made the requirements for price certainty even more critical. In the end Halifax and its partners came up with a solution that satisfied everyone's concerns.

Concannon explains how it was achieved "We had a link to Merrill Lynch so that we could execute trades automatically but interestingly not at the price they were necessarily quoting. We take an independent satellite price feed, which tells us what the best price is and Merrills have to match that". Girling tells us that "Merrill Lynch were very concerned about their exposure, because essentially they were doing all the retail trading in the Halifax shares. If a customer comes on the phone and they want to sell, we go and get them a quote, and that quote is valid for fifteen seconds. It is actually quite a long time when you are on the phone, but it is not very long to confirm details with customers because we had to read all the details back to them. But that is the price that the customer gets". Halifax had wanted a 30 second freeze on the price but it was reduced to 15 "on Merrills insistence" to reduce their exposure.

2.12 Bulk dealing

Another example of what might be termed lateral thinking was the bulk dealing system that Halifax introduced. Girling states, "Dealing initially in only a single stock made things easier, but it also meant that we could be much more efficient than anything our competitors would have. Our system is very cost efficient because we bulk all the trades up at the same price, and only execute them when certain limits have been reached or the price changes, and then we put them on the market as one big deal. So we might get 100 orders for 100 shares each, but on the market we would purchase 10,000 shares in bulk and that would save costs for us. We do one big deal, instead of a hundred small ones, so our CREST charges for settlement are in principle 100 time less. That's not the figure of course but substantial savings are made. And all that was quite clever and novel". He goes on to explain "if we have got ten customers on the phone, instantaneously buying and selling they will all get the same price. Now if the price changes that bulk would be closed and executed and another bulk started at the new price. The prices can be very volatile but if it stays at the same price for half an hour the bulks get to a certain size and then its closed because you have to be careful how you put the shares into the market, to avoid any accusations of sharp practices".

2.13 HSDL system

Turning now to some of the detail of HSDL we find that the use of the nominee system meant the Halifax could effectively re-engineer the share dealing process, introducing technology into what was traditionally a very intensive paper-based process. Girling emphasises the continuing focus on technology. He says, "the way you make money out of execution only share dealing is to perform a transaction for a customer and then they pay you a fee or a commission. There are not a lot of other ways of making money out of it. So doing it as efficiently as possible, and as quickly as possible, gives you an edge. The use of technology meant that we could take paper processes out of the equation and thus handle more volume at less cost".

2.14 The IT challenge

The task given to the IT department was to work on the creation of the new business, design a solution, and then acquire, test and implement the infrastructure and applications that formed the solution. The challenges that presented themselves were numerous. Firstly, the presence of an absolutely non-negotiable deadline, not one that the IT side of the business had any say in determining. Girling states that "the technology project was on the critical path, all the way through... there were other things like employing staff, and getting the skilled managers on the premises, but the technology was always the key issue". Secondly, the sheer magnitude of the volumes involved, and as has been stated these were outside the experience of any previous conversion. Thirdly, the fact that these volumes would present themselves on day one, rather than building up slowly over time, which would have provided some much needed breathing space and experience. Finally, there were really no people who were experienced in the business aspects of share dealing on board when the project was initiated, i.e. there were no business users. This meant that the IT side had to second guess the requirements for some considerable time and as indicated above those business users, including Concannon, did not come on board until relatively late in the day. Thus quite a considerable part of the system was designed and in place before the people who really knew the detail of the share dealing business and what was required had an opportunity to make an input.

2.15 IT/IS strategy

There were a number of elements to the strategy. The first was to build upon existing strengths. The Halifax Direct Call Centre system had been in place for 18 months and they built on the technology and experience of this. Thus one part of the picture would be a telephone based dealing service. Girling states, "we did have the call centre infrastructure, we didn't set this up from scratch. We took advantage of all the infrastructure that was already in place. All the automatic call distribution, the recording, the IVR (Interactive Voice Recognition) and CTI (Computer-Telephony Interface) capabilities were in place, they were actually using by touch-tone keystrokes to fire applications, we just exploited that".

The second element of the strategy was to identify a number of key external suppliers to provide the necessary major components together with a number of internally developed bespoke elements and interfaces. Girling says "We (the Halifax) were renowned for developing everything internally but we recognised that probably 60-70% of the solution existed in various places, we just needed to bring them together... So what we did was to take a number of industry standard components that were available, plus a share dealing administration system and we integrated them in a unique way. In order to do that we developed some bespoke software ourselves, and subsequently we developed a very efficient order capture and dealing mechanism just for Halifax shares".

Concannon, although not party to the decision making at that stage, comments on the approach, "the programme as a whole was so huge, with an absolute fixed end date, that the decision taken was very sensible. It was to do things that we had to do and look to external parties for things where they could bring additional expertise to the party. Quite a pragmatic approach really. Writing a stockbroking system from scratch is not really something you want to be doing really. It is relatively easy to develop for a straight forward transaction, but the minute you come across a dividend, or a capital event, or a rights issue, or a take over, or anything like that then it can be a complete nightmare. And of course there was lots of changes going on in the market place at the time, including CREST which was getting up and running at that stage". Thus the Halifax decided to contract with various key suppliers or partners for various elements of the system.

The first key partner was the Registrar. A registrar is an organisation that takes responsibility for maintaining a company's share register. Concannon says, "there were really only two to choose from, either Lloyds or RBS (Royal Bank of Scotland) and initial discussions were held with both parties. It soon became clear that RBS had by far the better attitude and approach from the Halifax perspective. Lloyds was very much doing things just the way they had always been done… whereas RBS were quite ahead and already exploring the electronic side of things, which we were so keen on." So the RBS were chosen and it was "an absolutely key partnership". They provided all the registrations and receiving bank activities, and obviously the company nominee system, which the Halifax systems linked directly into. They also did all the administration behind the nominee.

The second key partner was Merrill Lynch who were the principal retail Market Maker for Halifax shares. Market Makers are essentially wholesalers who provide both bid and offer prices for a particular stock ensuring that someone who wishes to trade can always find a buyer or seller. Merrill Lynch were one of Halifax's advisers and they had been joint brokers to the conversion offer. They were also the largest market maker in the UK and had a strong emphasis on retail business.

The third key partner was to be the software supplier. This was chosen via formal competition and Halifax issued an invitation to tender (ITT) in March 1996 to relevant companies. After an evaluation process, that included functional, technical and financial criteria, TCA Synergo were selected and a £2.5 million deal was entered into. TCA were well respected, independent suppliers of software to the securities and stockbroking sector, with major retail stockbroking clients. They had a product called TAROT which was their core electronic dealing and settlement system and it was a client-server rather than mainframe based architecture. Thus they had experience and credibility plus the kind of product Halifax were looking for. But additionally for Halifax they proposed to develop a special 'flotation' module that would interface with TAROT. The back office functions, e.g. settlement, contract note production, etc. would be undertaken within TAROT but the new module would streamline the order capture and execution facility, with links to RBSs nominee administration system and also to Merrill Lynch's execution dealing system. The module provided the capability to meet the Halifax's high volume requirements. Further, they suggested that when the initial high volumes had returned to more normal volumes and when Halifax moved to dealing the shares of other companies, the standard TAROT system would provide all the necessary longer-term functionality. TCA Synergo impressed with their good understanding of the unique nature of Halifax's requirements and their enthusiasm. They were chosen ahead of two other short-listed candidates.

2.16 ARIES system

The system that was developed was termed ARIES and from the perspective of a member wishing to sell their shares worked as follows:

They phoned HSDL and were greeted by a voice recognition system that asked various questions (including their 10 digit folio from the allocation of shares document, if they had it) and then it routed them to the next available relevant operator.

The folio number was then checked and verified via an interface with RBS in Bristol. RBS held the folio details, i.e. the nominee account, and then the details of the nominee would then be loaded to the operator's screen. The screen would then show the customers name, address, shares held, shares traded, etc.

If the customer was deemed eligible to trade, the current price at which they could sell would be displayed and the customer informed. This was obtained via the automated satellite feed provided by ICV.

A countdown timer would then start and the customer had 15 seconds to decide whether to sell, and if so how many shares. The price offered was frozen for that period and if the customer decided to sell within the 15 seconds the transaction was made and that would be the price they received. All calls were digitally recorded so that disputes or mistakes concerning the price stated or the number of shares to sell could easily be resolved.

Payment would then normally be made directly into the customers Halifax account but payment into another account via BACS or by cheque could be requested.

After the transaction the details were then sent back to RBS for updating of the nominee account. The individual trades were simply added to a current open bulk order which was only passed to Merrill Lynch when the price changed, or a maximum number or time limit was reached. A bulk order update then occurred, including updates to MAX (the Merrill Lynch system) and to TAROT so that the market settlement in CREST could be made. Various supporting batch activities also took place if necessary, such as cheque issuing, BACS payments, Debit card payments, CREST references, reports to the SFA, etc. In terms of Halifax technology the infrastructure consists of Unix based, HP machines installed at the data centres with large disk capacities, multiple servers and gateways, numerous communication links, interfaces to the various suppliers, PCs running Windows NT, and satellite links for the real-time price feeds, with the call centre running integrated voice and data CTI. The systems are also duplicated, including back-up generators, etc., at other sites and processing can be swapped from site to site if and when required. In terms of software development about 20% of the total was done in-house, including some internal applications, e.g. cheque processing, the Halifax Shareholder Account, various interfaces to supplier systems, and the desktop interfaces. These were primarily written in Visual Basic and utilised Oracle Databases.

2.17 Management and control of the project

The critical management issues concerned how to organise, integrate and control what was a multi-site, multi-supplier, multi-system project, with a deadline that simply could not be missed. To achieve this a highly formalised programme and project management system was put in place. This was essentially the approach that had been devised for the merger, under Miller, and as he was now responsible for the conversion, it is not surprising that essentially the same organisation and procedures were used as they had proven to work successfully. In connection to the merger, Miller comments that, "Almost every single job that has to be done affects others in the chain, so it's essential we organise it carefully. Even so, the approach is fairly straightforward. First, you design a programme of work which is watched over by the Programme Office, then you divide the work into manageable projects, and allocate small teams to deliver them". And this was essentially the process that was applied again.

There was a steering group for the whole conversion project which oversaw and co-ordinated all aspects. A number of programme charters were then established for each major part of the project and again a Programme Office was established to co-ordinate and plan the programmes and all the diverse elements of the overall project. The first programme concerned customer data quality (the clean-up of the member files), another concerned flotation and the share register, and yet another concerned share dealing. The Programme Office developed the high level plans and milestones for each programme and then each programme developed their own projects and plans within that. Miller states, "We introduced the Programme Office under Mike Channon, the Business Systems Manager, and we attempted to get a good understanding of architectures and structures and keep things away from each other as far as possible, i.e. separate things. We broke it down into mini projects, sub projects and tasks. And the programme office understood the inter-relationships... It was very formalised and rigorous".

Share dealing was broken down into project initiation, detailed requirements definition, solution design and development, testing, and pilot operation. Within this joint user and IT workshops were established involving all the partners and suppliers. These specified and agreed the detail of the business and systems requirements and established implementation plans, together with comprehensive issue and change management controls. Individual IT plans were established for core applications development, infrastructure installation, call centre development, integration of external and internal systems, and interfaces to external parties. In total 12 external technology suppliers and 8 internal project teams were used to deliver the various application and infrastructure components.

Concannon states that "We have quite a formalised project management process. It kicks off with the project implementation document which describes what we are doing and the project scope and project plan. Then there are the detailed requirements, business designs, requirements definition, test strategy, test plan, and implementation plan. Once the business designs have been signed off then they are very much a closed book and everything after that is done by change control. We have quite good issues management and change control processes. And we have stuck to these principles and procedures for all our subsequent development and they are now ingrained in the business."

Girling says that project management method is "very well defined, including definition of the project scope, responsibilities, quality plans, etc. The methodology really came from the old Leeds Permanent standards although they have been tweaked and improved since the merger. That is what we adhered to for the share dealing project. But it wasn't just for the technology project, we also had a recruitment project, a marketing project, a premises project, etc. All these projects worked to these same standards. There were about 15 sub-projects although the systems project was probably the biggest and on the critical path".

In relation to external suppliers Girling states that although Halifax had a very good project management method they felt they could not dictate its use to external suppliers and partners, "that would have been counter productive. So one of the criteria for picking suppliers was that they could demonstrate they had a methodology they could follow, including certain quality procedures. They were allowed to develop to their own standards and run their projects in their own way. What we insisted on was that they reported progress to us in a particular way that would meet our needs".

"We used to report fortnightly and I represented the systems project in the broader programme meeting. Here we used to talk about everything; recruitment, dealing, systems, infrastructure, so we all knew what was going on... The fortnightly report was very simple but very effective. It was a list of milestones, original dates, latest dates, and activities completed. Next it had a list of things achieved in the last 2 weeks, a list of things to be achieved in the next 2 weeks, and a set of issues for management attention. This highlighted the things that needed to be thrashed out. It was very simple and essentially we used it for the whole project".

"Managing the projects properly in this way was vital. In some cases when you tend to do the same type of project, time after time, then some of these deliverables tend to lose significance because they are always the same, but in a project like this it is very important because its so new and novel. For example, we had to give a lot of thought to testing and establish a test strategy. We had change control logs, we had issues logs, we had risk logs and impact logs, and we reviewed those every fortnight with the key suppliers. I chaired these meetings with the three project managers (from TCA Synergo, RBS and Merrill Lynch) to review progress and resolve issues. There was just the four of us and we developed a very close working relationship. We did that probably for nine months". These meetings rotated around the various venues. Girling says "We could have insisted that they all be held in Leeds but going to the various sites, seeing what was going on, getting to know each other, helped enormously".

Miller also acknowledges that dealing with external vendors complicated the management issue, he says, "we had to get everybody (internal and external) on the same wavelength, the same programme management review. We had to get them to recognise that they had a responsibility which was part of a larger undertaking. They had to appreciate that larger undertaking, and to play their part, along with other operations, so that everyone was effectively working together. Programme management forced that co operation".

But it was not just about procedures but also about culture. "We had to get the culture right. A culture of plain talking, and telling it as it was. Not trying to keep things under wraps. That way you don't get surprises. We solved a lot of problems just by straight forward plain talking and getting people to recognise the status of their particular activity". Miller says, "if we were getting less than we deserved from some organisation then I made it plain to them, and this happened on a couple of occasions. They were reverting back to their ways of working. What we kept saying to them was we don't want you to revert to your ways of working, we want you to embrace, collectively, our ways... In the end everybody played the game. They could see there was only a collective win. If you got the real time price feed up and working but you couldn't transact, it didn't help much. There was no such thing as an individual win". Girling reinforces this point and says that, "for some of the suppliers this was a major deal, it was their most important project. So these things were in our favour. People wanted it to happen and be successful. If it failed there would be serious repercussions all round, not just for us. They knew that".

The involvement of the external organisations and key partners was on the standard contractual basis, there were no special arrangements or bonuses, or reward-sharing schemes. "Just straight forward and professional" as Miller states. This was the case for both internal and external people. Although in fact there were some reward payments made after the event to internal people but as Girling says these were "out of the blue".

Apart from the importance of managing the project effectively the integration of IT and business people in the project was crucial. Miller says, "although technology was important we made sure that it wasn't an IS project... it was a business undertaking, that was vital. IS people were involved but they worked on a business project".

Concannon agrees saying, "The original project was set up very much as a joint working party looking at the options and right from the start business people and IT people worked in partnership. Then when the project was more formally kicked off, that process was continued, so that we had a business project manager, and a systems project manager who worked very much hand in hand. I think the IS staff... found it an enjoyable way to work as well. They liked understanding the business".

2.18 Testing

Testing was to be a key factor in the development of the service. As indicated this was not only a radically new business for the Halifax but it was a complex integration of systems involving external partners. There was the problem of volume, and there was the anticipated first day peak. All these factors pointed to the importance of testing, not just technology testing but business system testing. Recruitment and training was also important as around 140 new staff were employed in early 1997 to support the telephone based share dealing service and so testing would be about the whole business system from beginning to end. Concannon states, "We did endless testing. We put as much effort into testing as we did into design and development, I would say". And given the size of the design and development task this was a major effort.

There was of course testing of individual components and systems testing but on the approach to vesting day there was user acceptance testing (UAT), Model Office, Stress Testing and a Dress Rehearsal. User Acceptance Testing (UAT) commenced on January 6th to prove complete end to end processing and acceptance by the business users. Girling says, "We actually brought people into to act as shareholders, ring up on the phones, send correspondence in, we had dummy mail boxes, etc.". Incidents and queries were formally reported and change control requests activated. A major problem, as we have seen, is that for some considerable time there had been no real business users, i.e. the share dealing staff, for they had not yet been appointed. External consultants and others were used to help over come this problem but there is no substitute for real users. So User Acceptance Testing was the first real opportunity to get many of these new people involved. Indeed Girling states that it "was as much to exercise the new staff who had been trained as much as the system itself".

The next activity was termed the Model Office and lasted about four weeks. This was a scaled down and compressed run of the whole floatation, share registration and share dealing process. Then Stress Testing was performed, to test the systems with large volumes, and as the name implies, under stress. By then things were themselves getting stressed and Concannon recalls "that to fit it in the stress testers actually had to work shifts. It took longer than expected. They used a lot of stress testing tools to simulate the activity and at one point we brought in something like 100 users and got them all to log in at the same time, so we could see the impact".

Finally came the Dress Rehearsal, designed to trial the period from vesting day onwards. This involved live trading on the Stock Exchange, for which permission was obtained. Concannon says "We were live properly. We all bought a share in Lloyds, all at the same time so that we could see that it worked. The Stock exchange is very nervous about doing anything like that, even when doing small numbers of shares, it might be seen as manipulating the market, but they did agree to it. We had lots of external eyes on what we were doing all the time because the Stock Exchange, the regulators, etc. were all very concerned that we got this right and that it was going to work. We were literally crawled all over by auditors and regulators". The Dress Rehearsal also included testing difficult situations that might arise. Staff pretended to be awkward customers, saying things like, 'I haven't received this, this is wrong, what are you going to do about that'. The Dress Rehearsal ended on 23rd May, just two weeks before the big day. It was only then that the regulators gave their final approval to the Halifax to run their share dealing service. Concannon reflects that gaining the approval was "probably the most difficult area really. On the internal side, the systems, the development, the stuff we did internally, we had some control over, but with the regulator it was different. They would come and see us and we would provide them with all the information they requested and then they would come up with a whole new raft of requests. It was quite difficult and came right up to the wire before we got the final approvals".

2.19 Vesting Day

On Monday 2nd June 1997 the Halifax became a public limited company and 7.6 million eligible members received shares. On the Stock Exchange Halifax shares opened at 774.5p and closed at 735p with an average price that day of 732p. This meant that a Halifax member with the minimum share allocation had, in theory, a windfall of nearly £1,500 with the average per eligible member being £2,200. On that first day 1.9 million postal sale instructions were processed by HSDL. That is 23% of the members sold a total of 569 million shares, with over £3.5 billion automatically credited back to 1.6 million customers' accounts. The total value of the sale was £4.2billion, making it the largest trade ever on the London Stock Exchange. Additionally the telephone share dealing service received 8,000 calls and processed over 4,500 purchase instructions. The take up of the Halifax PEP was also a great success and it immediately became the country's largest single company PEP. The 23% of members selling their shares satisfied the institutional market (pre-vesting auction) down to bids of 711p, with the highest being 815p. The weighted average of the bids was 732.5p which was what selling members actually received. Concannon reflects that, "even quite late on we had no idea that the price would come out so high... 495p to 560p was the estimated range put in the Transfer Document... Yes, there was quite a lot of surprise around!". It is little wonder that the Consumer Confidence Index jumped by seven points and the Economist identified 'a new up beat mood' with almost every other household in the country experiencing 'the Halifax effect'. Apart from re-investment the impact was particularly felt in the travel and DIY industries, with many people spending their windfalls on holidays and improvements to their houses. The floatation was hailed as a great success and the Halifax Share Dealing Service was a major contributor to that success. System availability in the first week was 100% and they have continued to operate at extremely high levels since.

However, although implementation went very smoothly in general there was a problem on the first day with the telephone share dealing. According to Girling, "We had 100 users logged on the system, everything going well, and then we couldn't get the 101st logged on. RBS and TCA Synergo were on site for that day and within two minutes we knew what the problem was. A parameter had been set in the system to restrict it to 100 users for testing and it never got changed! It was a problem we couldn't solve until the system was bought down. So we had to run with it for the rest of the day. It was not early on that we hit the problem but sometime late in the morning. It did hit our capacity to handle calls, not significantly because we couldn't handle that many more than 100 people anyway. We did 4,500 trades that day and really it was fine. But it was a bit of a panic". In the end it was concluded that if that was the worst problem, as it was, then everything had gone alright! And what about the number of dissatisfied customers? The spectre of two Wembley Stadiums full of people had haunted the Board when they were considering the paper based share certificate route. Well in the end, according to Miller, there were only 167 of them, and most of these were dissatisfied with their share allocation rather than the share dealing system.

2.20 Post Vesting Day

Next the telephone share dealing service was extended to include the ability for members to sell Halifax shares as well as buy, and the service was soon regularly handling 6,000 plus customer orders a day. This had originally been scheduled for two months after vesting day but it was in place within two weeks. In November 1997 a certificated selling service was introduced enabling people who had not opted for the nominee account to sell their shares. As Girling says, "We did this because we were getting so many calls saying will you sell my shares but I took the certificate option. The demand was there and we were in a position to do it".

By January 1998 HSDL were handling greater daily volumes of deals than their major competitors but with 25-30% fewer order taking staff, indicating that their end-to-end processes were very efficient and effective. Over 2.6 million postal deals had been completed and 514,000 telephone deals, with average call times of only 2.5 minutes. Customer satisfaction was high with dealing errors at a low 0.01% and complaint level at 0.1% of deals, compared to the industry average of around 1%. Of course it can be argued that error rates should be low when you are only dealing in a single stock, nevertheless overall the rates are still impressive. Concannon felt that "generally people were very satisfied with the service that we offered... and it has been extremely well received... we also had high levels of referrals to other customers, which is a good sign".

In September 98, just over a year after conversion, Halifax launched ShareXpress, their all UK share dealing service. This was also nominee based but the nominee was this time held by the Halifax as the nominee. The disadvantage for the customer is that they can only sell shares bought in this way through the Halifax, although of course this is an advantage to the Halifax. Then the range of instruments that could be traded was expanded to include gilts, trusts, investments, etc. A self-select ISA was also launched, to enable people to shelter their shares from tax. In December 1998 a touch tone service for the Halifax Shareholder Account (HSA) was introduced. The system automatically deals with trades into and out of the HSA. When the instructions are entered by the customer via the phone the system reads back the details, asks for confirmation of the order, and executes the deal. So, as Girling says, "A customer can press a few buttons on their phones, get all the same information they do if they are talking to a human being, they get the real price and the settlement date and the amount. And during busy periods the touch tone service copes with over half our trades".

Finally in October 1999 Halifax launched its online banking and share dealing service, called Halifax-online. A customer registers with Share Xpress register over the phone and then they can use the internet service to deal. According to Girling, this has been "hugely successful in terms of volumes. We have done 20 times the target volumes and we had done all of this years business by end of last year! We are doing over 40% of our all stocks dealing via the internet now".

All these developments were essentially extensions to the original share dealing service and as Concannon states, "we have built on what we did originally in these subsequent programmes and we have used essentially the same project management processes, with the business and IS working in partnership. It has been extremely successful and it has established the Halifax in the mainstream of modern banking and share dealing provision". She goes on to reflect that, "being able to start with a clean piece of paper and being able to do something using the latest technology has been a big benefit to us. And even now, with all the interest there is in internet share dealing, we're one of only two companies in the UK that do proper on line, real time, straight through processing transactions on the internet".

Girling, says that "all the systems and architecture that we put in place at conversion have allowed us to develop the touch tone dealing, the all stocks dealing, and the internet dealing. We are in a position to continue as well, we could add interactive TV, mobile telephony, whatever we want, to this architecture, when the time is right". According to Miller apart from saving £9 million for the Halifax, which was the difference between the costs of having the initial share issue done by the city institutions and the cost of HSDL doing it, it is now a valuable business in its own right. The outcome of that early decision to abandon the paper trail, to focus on electronic trading, and to go for their own share dealing service, has been impressive. The result is a growing revenue stream, a capability for the future, and a much enhanced profile for the Halifax.

2.21 Lessons

Clearly each case is different and no two situations are really the same. Nevertheless there are perhaps some general lessons that might prove useful. It is hoped that the simple ones are clear from the above case but we would like to highlight the following.

Probably the first lesson of the Halifax is the importance of their 'can do' attitude, which is seen in many different contexts. A clear example is the decision not to accept the traditional approach to share dealing, as well as the search for new ways to organise, or re-engineer, the processes, despite their lack of experience in that domain. To some extent they were pushed into this by the large volumes but they had the confidence to do it. This was mainly a function of the people involved and the climate and culture that was engendered.

For the Halifax the project management procedures and standards that had been used for the merger were obviously of critical importance. Managing such a large and disparate project without very good organisation and procedures in place would have been problematic. It was not just the detailed procedures but the overall approach that was important. Breaking the project down into its constituent parts (programmes) and then keeping them separate as far as possible with the Programme Office responsible for co-ordination was important to the success. As Miller stated it is simple in principle but few people actually do it. The formal procedures and reporting systems have to be followed closely but it was not just the fact that these were in place but that they were well understood and as Concannon says 'ingrained'. Although the project management procedures were rigorous and formalised they were not used to substitute or push out the informal communication. There was also lots of informal and face to face communication as well, 'we talked, discussed issues, and worked together'. It was the procedures and experience and confidence in using them that enabled Halifax to attempt the undertaking, despite the difficulties. As Girling says, "we weren't the world experts in share dealing but we knew we could run a project like this".

Given this emphasis on the Halifax project method it is perhaps surprising that they did not force these procedures on their suppliers and partners. Although of course it would have been difficult as they did not have the experience of them. So it was sensible to let the suppliers use their own methods and trust them to deliver. What they did do was to ensure that the reporting and communication of progress was done in the way that Halifax wanted. The risk was minimised to some extent because, as Girling says, as part of the selection process we ensured that the suppliers did have what were regarded as good methodologies and standards, even if they were not ours.

The effective integration of the IT and the business was another critical factor, it was not an IT project but a new business undertaking. Such IT and business integration is often talked about and recognised as important but much more rarely achieved. The fact that initially they did not have any business users might have forced the IT people to play that role to some extent, and may have helped with the integration. But whatever the reasons it was achieved and as we have seen Miller thought it an important success factor and having this driven from the top is always helpful. It is very interesting that Concannon tells us that "today we actually cross over with project planning, so for one project the systems people would do the planning, then the next one will be planned by the business people. Just to make sure that we are passing the skills around. It is very much a joint process, and if there are any issues or problems, any particular item comes up, it's a joint discussion on what we are going to do about it". Girling stresses that the IT being co-located with the business dealing side was also important in this regard.

The development of the share dealing business using a range of suppliers with three as key partners was important. It was not just that it had to be done by the deadline but the recognition that 60-70% of the solution already existed 'out there'. This was not simply using standard packages but taking existing software and integrating it in 'clever and novel' ways. The problem with standard packages is that others can buy them and any advantage is negated or that any developments the vendor does for you finds its way into the market place. But, as Concannon says, we did about 20% of the development ourselves, developing our own interfaces with other systems, user interfaces, etc. It meant we did some of the clever stuff, on the desktop rather than in the main system. We certainly feel this gave us an advantage, better control and a more central relationship".

Although this was a completely new business for the Halifax the requirements were effectively established by around the middle of 1996 and were quite stable from then on. Defining the business requirements took a lot of effort, a lot of teasing out, and a lot of discussion. This indicates that they did a good job, even without the presence of the business users, as we have seen, but the use of consultants and advisors worked well. Also once the requirements were signed off they were not expected to change, even when the business users came on board. Once established changing them was a major issue and a formal change control procedure was imposed. These two factors, getting the requirements as right as possible and then accepting only well justified changes, contributed significantly to achieving the objectives and were essential to meeting the deadline.

The project was seen as important and was well resourced by the organisation. The Halifax brand and reputation was of key concern and corners were not cut on the project, 'things were not done by half'. There was senior management backing and commitment which is always an important success factor. As Girling says, "John (Miller) was the champion. It was very much his baby and he provided the leadership". Strangely enough, although the implementation date was very challenging, in some ways it was thought to have contributed to the success of the project, 'because it focuses everybody's minds and provides a will to make things happen'. In the Halifax it was termed 'getting boulders off the runway' and the criticality of the date made this process easier. Additionally it made people, as we have seen, reluctant to ask for changes unless absolutely necessary.

In terms of developing the system although it was a new and challenging area for the Halifax they sensibly built on a number of existing strengths. They used the technology and their experience that already existed, for example, the telecommunications, the call centres and the helplines. As Girling says "we had a lot of technical expertise that we were able to bring to this project".

In such a new business the testing and confidence building was a key issue, and this the Halifax did very well. We have seen that the various strategies adopted such as Model Office, Stress Testing and the Dress Rehearsal. These were not just paying lip service to testing but very serious events, lasting many weeks each. For example, the Dress Rehearsal involved live running on the Stock Exchange, which was very difficult to organise but absolutely essential to prove that all the parts worked together. The emphasis on business system testing, rather than just IT systems testing, is also an important lesson, i.e. it is the whole business system, including the call centre, the operators, the satellite feeds, the partners, the dealers, etc. that has to work. If one part does not work then the whole thing fails. Afterwards it is no good saying "Oh well, our bit worked OK".

The approach to the system architecture was not just focused on the short-term requirement to trade in Halifax shares. It was always recognised that the longer-term capability was equally important and the potential for all share dealing and an internet channel was always in mind. This seems to have been a good example of vision and long-term planning. For example, the choice of TCA Synergo, was partly based on their understanding of, and capability of delivering, for the longer term.

The choice of a Unix based client-server architecture, a single architecture, interfacing to other systems, all these decisions were taken with the longer term requirements in mind. And, as indicated above, this is still holding them in good stead because they can easily deal with 'mobile telephony, EMU, interactive TV, and whatever appears on the horizon. As Girling says, "the architecture is a luxury which gives us an advantage over most of our competitors… they have to run multiple systems and deal with legacy".

2.22 References

[1] Pugh, P. (1998) The Strength to Change: Transforming a Business for the 21st Century, Penguin Books, Harmodsworth.

[2] Keasy, K., Hudson, R. and Littler, K. (1998) The Intelligent Guide to Stock Market Investment, John Wiley & Sons, Chichester.

Chapter 3

The London Ambulance Service Computer Aided Dispatch (LAS-CAD) System

3.1 Introduction

It is well known that the computer systems associated with the dispatch of ambulances in the London Ambulance Service (LAS) have had a chequered history. Indeed the 1992 Computer Aided Dispatch (CAD) system has become widely known as a prime example of an information systems failure [1] [2] [3]. However, it is less well known that prior to this there was another CAD system failure. In the autumn of 1990 a system provided by IAL (a subsidiary of BT) was scrapped just before implementation due to problems relating to 'load test performance criteria' (Page, 1993) at a cost of £7.5million. Having had two failures what were the chances of getting a third attempt to computerise the dispatch system to be successful?

In October 1992 the second attempt at a computer-aided dispatch (CAD) system at the London Ambulance Service failed. Following a significant slowdown and failure to reliably dispatch ambulances, the system had to be replaced with manual procedures for taking and recording calls and dispatching emergency vehicles. This failure hit the national headlines with suggestions that 20-30 people died as a result [4], indeed as also reported in the Guardian NUPE's London regional organiser suggested that the system over its short life had been responsible for 45 deaths. Many Londoners remember the events with horror [3] and many recall phoning the emergency ambulance service to be greeted with a recorded message [2]. In fact the reported death toll was greatly exaggerated by the press and the public enquiry (Page, 1993) that followed suggested that it was likely that no deaths could be blamed on the system. Nevertheless the failure was clearly a disaster for the LAS with the credibility of the service in tatters and for the people of London who felt extremely vulnerable. The fact that nobody died was good fortune rather than an indication that the system failure was not a catastrophe.

3.2 Background of the London Ambulance Service (LAS)

Historically the first full time ambulance service was established in London in 1897. An Act of Parliament, the Poor Law, set up the Metropolitan Asylums Board (MAB). It founded asylums for sick, insane or infirm people. From 1867 until 1930 the MAB ran several hospitals and an ambulance service to convey its own patients from their homes to hospital. In 1930 the work of the MAB was transferred to the newly formed London County Council (the effective establishment of the LAS). With the coming of the National Health Service (NHS) in 1948 it was made a duty for ambulances to be available for those who needed them, and this still applies today, i.e. it is a legal duty for ambulances to be available if requested. In 1965 with the establishment of the GLC (Greater London Council) the service was reorganised with one ambulance service being formed in London from all or parts of nine existing services. In 1974 the service was transferred from local government to the responsibility of the South West Thames Regional Health Authority (RHA) with the NHS reorganisation of the day. Further changes led to the LAS becoming an NHS Trust in 1996.

The current LAS is the largest ambulance services in the world and its area of responsibility covers 7 million people, although its daytime population is larger particularly in Central London, and covers an area of 620 square miles. The LAS has two main functions, the Accident and Emergency Service (A&E) and the Patient Transport Service (PTS). The PTS is concerned with transporting patients to and from hospital for appointments as outpatients at clinics, day centres and day surgery units. These are non-emergency patients who are medically unable to travel by public transport. These Services are provided by the LAS for the hospitals and are paid for by the hospitals. The dispatch system for PTS is computer controlled but is completely separate from the emergency service system. The LAS comprises 70 ambulance stations, 700 vehicles (around 400 ambulances, plus helicopter, motorcycles, and other patient transfer vehicles) and over 3,000 people (670 paramedics, 300 control staff). On average, the A&E Service responds to 2,500 calls per day (1,500 of which are 999 calls) with PTS making around 3,800 journeys per day. The demand for emergency services has increased steadily over the years with an annual growth rate of 16% in some years.

3.3 The story of the 1992 failure

As indicated above the story of the 1992 collapse is quite well known but it will be briefly re-stated here to form the context for the new system.

Beynon-Davies [1] reports that on the night of Monday 26th October 1992 "a flood of 999 calls apparently swamped operators' screens... and that many recorded calls were wiped... causing a mass of automatic alerts to be generated, indicating that calls to ambulances had not been acknowledged". The operators were unable to deal with the messages that the system was producing and unable to clear the queues that developed. These queues slowed the system and increasingly when ambulances completed a job they were not cleared. Thus the system had fewer and fewer resources to allocate. This eventually caused the system to enter what Beynon-Davies characterised as a 'vicious circle of cause and effect' which "cumulatively led to all the symptoms of systems failure" (Page et al., 1993). The system knew the correct location and status of fewer vehicles, resulting in duplicated and delayed allocations, a build up of exception messages and the awaiting attention list, and an increased number of call backs and hence delays in telephone answering. Exception messages scrolled off the tops of the screens and it was difficult for the operators to retrieve them. Any that were not dealt with generated more exception messages. At one point a decision was taken to wipe the exception report queue in an effort to clear the system but unfortunately this probably had the effect of generating even more exception messages.

The result was chaos in the emergency service, multiple vehicles appear to have been sent to some incidents and none to others. Sometimes the closest vehicle was not the one dispatched. Crews reported ambulances from far afield passing them on the way to a call for which they were better placed. Crews began querying allocations and requesting information, which led to an increase in radio traffic and radio bottlenecks, which further delayed things. It is reported (Fink & Dowell, 1996) that in one case an ambulance arrived to find the patient dead and taken away by undertakers and another where an ambulance answered a stroke' call after 11 hours to find that the patient had made their own way to hospital! The crews were very frustrated as of course they took the brunt of the usually angry reaction from the public when they did turn up.

The system staggered on over the long hours of Monday 26th October and on into Tuesday 27th but was clearly not viable although it is said that it never collapsed completely. Finally at 2pm on the 27th LAS reverted to a semi-manual method of operation. Calls continued to be taken on the system (including use of gazetteer) but the incident details were printed out and allocation was done manually (as prior to the new system). Mobilisation of ambulances was then done via the system. This, together with an increase in the number of allocating staff for each shift, proved relatively successful and the Page Report states that "In general CAC staff were comfortable with operating this system as they found the computer based call taking and the gazetteer for the most part reliable. There were known inadequacies with the gazetteer and occasional "lock–up" problems with workstations, but overall the benefits outweighed the disadvantages. The vehicle crews were also more comfortable as the stations still had local flexibility in deciding which resource to allocate to an incident. The radio voice channels were available to help clear up any mobilisation misunderstandings... thus reducing significantly the average call waiting time."

Unsurprisingly the problems of the 26th and 27th October hit the newspaper headlines with a vengeance and questions were also asked in Parliament. The following day the LAS Chief Executive, John Wilby, resigned and Martin Gorham, deputy chief executive of South West Thames Regional Health Authority was appointed in his place, on a temporary basis. Shortly afterwards the Health Secretary, Virginia Bottomley, announced that there would be a public inquiry into the LAS, headed by Don Page, Chief Executive of South Yorkshire Metropolitan Ambulance Service.

Unfortunately, the semi-manual system did not last long either. On 4th November 1992 the system failed to print out calls and shortly after this LAS reverted to a fully manual, paper based system, with voice or telephone ambulance mobilisation. Luckily no serious ramifications were reported as this occurred in the early hours of the morning, nevertheless it was a further blow to the beleaguered LAS. The Times of 5 November 1992 reported a 25 minute delay in dispatching an ambulance and that senior management were forced to "concede that the system could not cope with its task".

In operational terms the LAS was now back to where it was prior to the 1992 system, i.e. manual operation using pen and paper. This continued essentially until the introduction of the new CAD system in 1996 although a number of background changes were being introduced. The manual system appeared to be working reasonably well, indeed it was reported in the Guardian (seven months after the collapse of the CAD system) that "the ambulance service is achieving its highest-ever response times thanks to the humble pen and paper".

3.3.1 Outcome of the Inquiry

The report of the Page Inquiry was published in February 1993 with further consequences. The Chairman of the LAS Board resigned and the Board itself was dissolved with the LAS returning to being directly managed by the South West Thames Regional Health Authority (RHA). The Report was a substantial piece of work and made some important statements concerning the CAD failure but perhaps more importantly made a series of conclusions and recommendations for the LAS for the future. Interestingly, and despite the problems, LAS was recommended to continue to seek a computer solution for ambulance dispatch but that "it must be developed and introduced in a time scale which, whilst recognising the need for earliest introduction, must allow fully for consultation, quality assurance, testing, and training" (Page, 1009). In relation to the management of LAS a restructuring was recommended together with a range of new appointments including a project manager and an IT Director. Significantly it was acknowledged that many of the recommendations had resource implications and the South West Thames RHA was encouraged to devise a financial strategy that accommodated this.

3.3.2 The arrival of the new Chief Executive

Gorham's introduction as CEO of LAS was memorable. He was appointed the day after Wilby, the previous CEO resigned, in a flurry of media interest. He was a career NHS manager, and had been in the NHS for about 25 years, mainly in hospital management and had been director of corporate planning for a large health authority. At the time he was the deputy regional general manager of South West Thames RHA and was involved with the implementation of the then new NHS reforms being driven by Kenneth Clarke, the Health Minister in the conservative government of Margaret Thatcher. Essentially Gorham had been introducing and managing change in hospitals and health services for most of his career.
Gorham states,

"I actually knew very little about the LAS before the event... it wasn't part of my remit. However, it became apparent to me during the middle of 1992 that things were clearly seriously amiss... The modernisation programme that was being pursued was not having the desired results, and there was this difficult history of very poor industrial relations which had rather come to a head.

I was asked about a fortnight before the computer collapse whether I would be willing to 'caretake' the LAS if the chief exec was in a position where he couldn't go on. It was getting to the point where it was becoming untenable for him to stay in the post. After some initial reluctance, we actually struck the deal the night the computer was collapsing, although we didn't know it at the time. It was said that it would probably be about Christmas the way things are going... Of course, the next morning I woke up to the news that the computer had failed. And then I got a call in the car around lunchtime to say did I want this job? And by the way, could I get myself there because the Secretary of State was due to announce it in the House? By 6 o'clock in the evening I was in the post and on national television!"

Gorham first set about making sure minimum management arrangements were in place that would hold things together. He then tried very rapidly to learn the service by getting out and meeting people and stressing the basic messages. He was keen to establish a period of stability and retrenchment. He clearly stated that he was not going to be rushed into changing things, that he recognised that the Service had been through a period of enormous, very uncontrolled change. He calculated that people needed a break as they were totally shell-shocked, the last thing he wanted to do was to be rushed into another ill-thought out scheme. He spent quite some time in the central control room, because that is where it had happened and describes the staff as being "in an awful state. They'd all worked very, very hard to make the thing work, and it had just sort of blown up in their hands. It was like after a bomb, really". He also spent time with the ambulance crews and went out with them on calls, a learning process for him and quite a shock for the crews! At this time the dispatch system was continuing to operate on a manual basis.

3.3.3 Dealing with the unions

One of the other things Gorham did was to talk to the union representatives and try and establish some kind of relationship and dialogue. He saw their role as crucial and needed them to be, if not completely supportive, at least not too antagonistic. He set out his stall by saying "I'm not really here for a battle with the trade unions. I'm here to ensure the future of the LAS and I'm sure that's what you're here for too and we'll achieve it a lot quicker, and a lot better, working together rather than continuing this highly public confrontation". Although at the time this seemed a vain hope, given the previous history of conflict. There had been a very damaging pay dispute before the current CAD problems and the ramifications were still evident. Although the dispute had eventually been resolved at a national level the London area had voted against the settlement which the rest of the country had agreed. Although, according to Gorham, he felt working together was not impossible because the unions were apparently quite shocked at the turn of events, particularly the resignation of Wilby. They had seen him as the problem and now found themselves having 'won' that battle but not quite knowing where to go next. In a sense they now needed Gorham as much as some other people needed him, otherwise they had no frame of reference, which Gorham describes as 'quite useful'!

Nevertheless it could have gone either way. Very early on the union representatives came into Gorham's office and demanded that the computer system be switched off completely. At the time the semi-manual system was in operation. Gorham admits he did not really know what to do. He had the unions on one side saying it must be shut down and what was left of his management team telling him that to shut down would be the final abdication. He says "there I was sat in the middle and didn't actually understand what they were talking about anyway". In fact he managed to buy some time by going to the unions London regional officer to get the staff to back off for a few days which they did.

On the management side Gorham found himself with a Director of Support Services, called Allen Kennedy, and a Director of Operations. The director of operations was on sick leave, so Kennedy was actually acting as director of operations as well. In effect he was the project manager for the computer project in the control room. He'd been overloaded and working very hard. However, because of his project manager role he was associated with the system and was seen as the next hate figure for the unions. Gorham says that in this context he made "one of those snap judgements that with the benefit of hindsight turned out to be a very good one". He decided that he was not going to move Kennedy because he had experience and Gorham needed that for the next phase. Also he felt he could not have the unions deciding who should stay and who should go. As it turned out Kennedy proved 'exactly the right person to keep the show on the road while I did my job'. Gorham could not afford to get sucked into very heavy levels of detail, which would have happened had Kennedy not been there. Gorham had to start taking control of the big decisions and directions.

3.3.4 The Nasima Begum Case

Meanwhile the manual system continued to operate until a new CAD system could be implemented and, as indicated above, was thought to be working reasonably well. But this was not the case, for in June 1994 the LAS was again "blown off course" by the tragic case of Nasima Begum, an 11 year old girl, who died after "being denied an ambulance" [2]. Nasima Begum had a liver condition for which she was receiving regular treatment but on this day her condition required urgent attention. Unfortunately despite four calls she had to wait 53 minutes for the ambulance only to die of renal failure. The tragedy was compounded by the fact that she lived only two minutes from a hospital and that the only available ambulance was sent elsewhere, to someone that did not really require emergency service. Again, and unsurprisingly, very bad publicity resulted, particularly with the death attributed by many to the delay in dispatching an ambulance. The case resulted in another review of the Service, this time by William Wells, South West Thames RHA Chairman, on behalf of the Secretary of State. This review underlined the Page Inquiry recommendations and introduced more initiatives. Further, in the first part of 1995 the House of Commons, through their Select Committee on Health, carried out their inquiry into the Service and commented "that lives may well have been lost".

The LAS had been 'digested and spat out in inquiry terms' and became something of a political football with the problems of the LAS a hot topic at the party political conferences in October of that year. Gorham says of that time that "it was awful and it felt to people who had been around for the previous event, 'Oh god, we're right back where we started' and I wondered, 'how long I was going to survive?'".

2.3.5 The genesis of the new CAD system

A new computer based system had been recommended by the Page Report and most of the subsequent investigations into the LAS also called for a computer system to be adopted, but what they wanted mostly was for something to be seen to be done and done quickly. Virginia Bottomley stated that "the tragic death of Nasima Begum in deplorable circumstances was a graphic reminder that much more needs to be done to improve the performance of the London Ambulance Service". The Select Committee considered that the LAS management was "open to severe criticism for not having moved faster". The political pressure was enormous. However, Gorham and his team felt strongly that to introduce a new computer system quickly was likely to lead to at least some of the same problems that had afflicted the 1992 system. He felt that the risk was too high and so adopted a very cautious approach, despite the political pressures, seeking to win hearts and minds, before considering publicly any new computer system. The fact that a new system would have to be introduced at some point was not in doubt. The increasing volumes of calls and the performance levels that were being demanded by the government meant that a manual system was not viable in the long term. The manual system, at its best, after the crash, had touched levels where 70% of calls were responded to within 14 minutes, however, the Patient's Charter required the level to be 95% which was considered not possible with a manual system. On top of this demand for the service was increasing steadily. After the crash Gorham had made sure that more staff were available to support the manual system, and this definitely helped, but slowly the workloads started creeping up again after having been stable for a couple of years. Unfortunately this meant that as new staff came on board the results, which were not particularly good anyway, stood still. This was very frustrating to everyone and made it seem that no progress was being made. As Ian Tighe, the new IT Director, commented "Most observers were certain that change should come far quicker than it was, and at times it was very hard to resist the pressure to dash into early change". However, resist it they did.

3.3.6 The foundations

Tighe states that he spent "nine months really just listening to people, and only dealing with those things that were desperately urgent. The rest of the time I just learnt about the service, what it was and what it did, how people did things, what gave them concerns. So that when you sit down with people and talk about bringing in change, you're doing so from a position of some knowledge, not definitive knowledge, but some knowledge and you understand what they do and how they do it. At the end of this period I produced a strategy document specifying what I felt we should do next, given what we know, given the past, this is what we should do, and this is how we do it". In outline the strategy for a new system advocated reducing the complexity of operation, concentrating upon key deliverables, paying attention to staff and their needs, establishing a workable but acceptable pace for delivery and implementation and, finally, it was to be built upon a number of prior infra-structure changes.

3.3.7 Infrastructure

During Tighe's listening period it became clear that in some ways the replacement of the CAD system was the least of his worries. He quickly discovered that the electrical supply was unsafe, that the switchboard was dying on its feet, and that the existing Control Room was such a mess that it probably could not just be refurbished but would require a new one to be built. On top of this the ambulance fleet was ageing and becoming difficult to maintain. It was obvious that the LAS had been suffering from under-investment, not just prior to the crash, but over many years. With these problems to face a new CAD system seemed quite a distant prospect because without updating the infrastructure it was quite likely that any new CAD system would fail due to these other factors. Thus Gorham and Tighe embarked on a series of what they termed 'warm-up' projects. These were things that needed doing, would provide some immediate benefit, but most of all, if they were undertaken well and successfully would lead to the re-establishment of management credibility and pave the way for a new CAD system.

First the electrical supply system was addressed and the HQ complex was completely rewired. The next project dealt with the emergency telephone system itself and replaced the old exchange with a digital system in April 1995. The electrical supply is a vital part of the emergency 999 calls system and as this was the first technological project to be delivered since the 1992 crash it was felt that many observers were waiting for the Service to trip up again. This was not to be the case and the project went smoothly providing the new management with an important success.

Tighe had undertaken a major installation of a digital exchange previously in the West Midlands Police so he felt he knew how to make this successful. "If you have some experience of large scale change you get to know how minor concerns and niggles can become great big problems if you don't address them". A great deal of effort was devoted to taking the people along with what was happening. For Tighe it was about asking "Well, why didn't it work before? The technological aspects had always spelt trouble but if we ignore that side, why did people reject it? How do we generate a different reaction? Can we create a different environment where people are actually more willing to accept that change is actually positive, that there is something in it for them as well as for everybody else". So for example, in relation to the digital telephony they talked to the call takers, and played them some of the old tapes (all conversations with the public are recorded) and asked them if they understand every word that was said. Well they thought they did but it was clear that some interpretation was taking place. "Then we would play them a digital tape and they would say 'yeah, I got every word of that, thanks', and they began to see that there was something in it for them. That they were less likely to come under investigation because they got an address wrong or there was a delay on a vehicle being dispatched".

The new digital PABX/Automatic Call Distribution System, together with DAT (Digital Audio Tape) recording of all calls and radio traffic, was successfully introduced in April 1995. It provided immediate improvements in the reliability of the system and the quality of the sound for the call takers, together with reduced support costs. Tighe says "This was a 'warm-up' project for us along with in May 1995 the replacement of various parts of the radio system to give greater capacity and better coverage. These worked well and people began to gain confidence in us, they saw that we actually did know a little bit about technology". "On top of this we were also building the new control room (CAC, Central Ambulance Control). We were starting from scratch in terms of the construction and engineering works, which made this something of a green field project, all the rest were upgrades of the existing system. It was great to be able to build that and put cable trays in and test the cabling and so on, with no impact upon users".

Over the period about half the ambulance vehicles were replaced, reducing the average age of a vehicle to 18 months. The fleet was old and the design of the ambulances not much liked by the crews. Particularly one that the previous Chief Executive had introduced that didn't have a connecting door between the cab and the back of the ambulance. Avril Hardy, the Training and Development Manager, and someone who lived through the troubled times, states "there was a lot of fuss about that, understandably. London's a dangerous place. You wouldn't want to be that far from your crew mate". So a process of involving people was undertaken and the crews were asked what they considered to be the best type of vehicle for the job. As Tighe states, "The vehicle is just a tool after all, you know, you would give a brick layer freedom to choose his own trowel, because you want him to do a good job and that's is all we did. Although it's a £50,000 trowel! Over a number of years we have replaced the vehicles and gone to a more powerful petrol driven vehicle, with doors where they want them with automatic transmission, and air-conditioning in the cabs, because we want them to sit around on sunny days on standby when there's no station. We've done those things, now we're not there yet with crews. They still don't like everything that's in their working life but we've made tremendous efforts to say well if you've got to do it you might as well be comfortable when you're doing it".

A good example of this was the provision of the crews with hand portable radios in 1995 so they could be in communication with each other and the control room even when away from their vehicles, whereas previously they had to return to the vehicle to get in touch. This saved time but the unit was also designed to increase staff security with the provision of an emergency button to press if they encountered trouble. This gave something of benefit directly to the crews.

A big issue arose concerning uniforms in the service. The existing uniform had been imposed by the previous management and crews really hated it. Gorham decided to change it but it caused enormous debate. There were people who were signed up to the existing uniform and vowed never to give it up. There were people who wanted to go back to a previous uniform, and that was the only thing they were going to accept. People were in corners and it became a real issue. Eventually a compromise was achieved. Gorham says it was "the uniform that they currently wear, but the colour of the previous one, but more like the style of something else! It was tricky stuff, very emotive, and very expensive, of course. To some outsiders, it might have seemed a bit like 'pissing while Rome was burning'. In terms of the culture of the Service, and re-capturing the morale and commitment and their self-image, it was terribly important to try and get it right".

3.3.8 Management structure

Meanwhile, in response to the Page inquiry, Gorham developed an action plan that included a new management structure with new appointments. It had become obvious to him that a substantial restructuring of the LAS was required.

"I said to people at the time and I meant it, that ideally I would not have wanted to restructure, because the last thing you need to do when you're in that kind of situation is to start playing with the pieces. I mean, there's work to be done, but the simple fact was that the current structure was a complete obstacle to making progress. We didn't have the level of management resources that we needed. I think that's one of the reasons why my predecessor wasn't able to deliver what he set out to deliver. He just never had the high level management resources you need to turn around a big high-profile, complex organisation which had drifted 10-15 years behind the time".

Gorham advocated to a four divisional structure. This proved controversial because one of the divisions he created was a Central London division, and people immediately assumed that that was a device to break the LAS up. To some it looked as if Gorham was suggesting that Central London would remain as LAS responsibility but that the outlying divisions would be absorbed into their neighbouring services, which in fact had always been one of the options that had been touted around. According to Gorham this was not his objective, "It was vastly more controversial than I expected, God knows why, I never understood why the neighbouring services would want part of the LAS, they could never have coped with it... just the Central London division was bigger by any reasonable measure than any other ambulance service in England!"

Nevertheless it did prove quite difficult. It actually drifted on for a couple of years and eventually was subject to a sort of formal grievance because Gorham eventually imposed it and it was one of the few times that he did not compromise when something was not popular. He states that to him it was clear that "we needed top flight managers for the divisional posts, and we needed top flight people in support posts". He obtained the support of the RHA together with the resources and got on with it. He made seven appointments of Directors including the Divisional Directors, an IT Director, a Personnel Director and a Finance Director. The divisional directors were all very experienced ambulance executives, indeed the appointment for the Central Division was Don Page, the Chair of the public inquiry. According to Gorham, "He did the report, and then came and did the job". The Executive Board now consisted of the Chief Executive (Gorham), a Deputy Director (Kennedy), a Finance Director, a Personnel Director, an IT Director (Tighe), an Operations Director, and the four divisional directors. Then the next phase of the restructuring was for each Divisional Director to develop the sort of supporting structure they needed.

3.3.9 New rosters

Gorham also came to the conclusion that the existing staff rostering system was not helping deliver the kind of service that was needed. He says, "The cover was wrong. We were still working on traditional rosters, which meant that we had far too many crews in the wrong place and there wasn't nearly enough cover on evenings and weekends". But this was not calculated to go down well with the staff, indeed a battle about rosters had been going on for many years, and epitomised the poor industrial relations of the LAS.

New rosters were devised based on research commissioned by LAS to identify patterns of demand and ways of matching resources to that demand. The outcomes were to keep ambulances within clearly defined local working zones, to match the deployment of ambulances with the established pattern of demand, to have some ambulances stand on the streets at critical locations, away from the stations, and to change the working patterns to reflect the demand at different times of the day and week. The staff voted against it, which indicated, despite some improvements, the continuing problems with management/staff relations. However, the majority against was too small to result in any real support for industrial action. So Gorham went ahead and pushed through the new rosters. He describes it as "very difficult and a bit surreal! The vote had been lost, and yet we were saying how do we go ahead and implement these new schemes anyway". The rosters were pushed through but started to show benefits quite rapidly.

So although no computer system had been introduced many of the necessary infrastructure changes had been made. Each providing a degree of benefit in their own right but not enough on their own. So the final piece of the strategy was the new CAD system. With this it was hoped that the big productivity benefits would accrue and that the performance measures set by the Government could be achieved.

3.3.10 The new CAD system

A new hardware platform was chosen for the system. The old system was essentially a PC architecture, which was not thought to be up to the job. The new system was to be UNIX based with Informix as the database software, supporting 60 workstations. According to Tighe, "We took the safe solution, this has worked for 20 years in other emergency services, and we know it works, and for us safety was the number one priority". The dispatch software itself was written in the C programming language and developed in-house. A review of what was available in the dispatch market place had been undertaken but the conclusion was that the packages were inadequate for the LAS. The strategy was to implement the system slowly in small simple chunks without having the full range of command and control facilities available, in essence a prototype approach. The packages available in the market place all did much more than wanted initially and the functionality could not be separated and presented in phases. Tighe states "We wanted to control the pace of change, we didn't want to be in the position that to carry out a simple function you had to know about ten others, because that would have changed the pace. We needed to dictate the agenda". Beyond that they did not mirror closely enough the way that the LAS wanted to organise dispatch. They did not want to be forced into a particular way of working because a package demanded it. Given the history the system had to be acceptable to the staff and according to Tighe, "the only thing they would find acceptable is the thing that they invent. That was the essence of it". Finally, although they never got to the point of testing it, there was a worry about a package coping with the large volumes required for the LAS.

3.3.11 Systems development

Once the decision had been made to develop in-house Quentin Armitage was appointed, also from West Midlands Police. Armitage did most of the actual programming with help form Tighe. Thus a very small development operation.

One of the principles concerning the new system was that it should initially be as close as possible to the functioning of the manual system, it should not introduce new ways of working. This was felt to be necessary because the staff were closely wedded to, and believed in, the existing manual ways. Also from their experience they were not enamoured with computers and felt that computers were not able to undertake dispatch tasks, or even aid in such tasks. The way forward was to be a duplication, as far as possible, of the manual system, with the opportunity to enhance this, once the system was in place and accepted. As Hardy states, "We wanted everything to be the same, the screen format was to follow as closely as possible what prints out on paper and the printed version of the call should also be the same format that would be used if you were hand writing". Again history was very influential here, with the old, failed, computer system the screen layout was nothing like the paper format. People not only had to learn how to do both things but when the computer went down or, problems were encountered, it was very hard for people to swap between the two, and this had caused significant problems. Another difference was in terms of project management. The previous system had specified that PRINCE (a project management method) should be used but the developers appointed did not know PRINCE and therefore it was not really followed. PRINCE exception reports were never raised because of the fear of delivering bad news. This time it was different PRINCE was used as the main project driving method but the culture had to be changed to make it work. Tighe states, "we had to convince people that if they saw a problem that they must not feel ashamed and think that they have made a mistake that they must hide. We had to instil the understanding that the problems had to be aired and that they could be put right. But you must tell us about them because we want to address them". It had to be an open culture that revealed 'warts and all'. This could only be achieved in relation to the development of the system because the culture of the whole organisation was also changing. The project management method was used throughout, so everyone understood it, the reports required, the project assurance team, the significance of it, etc. It began with the warm-up projects and thus people knew about it long before the computer system was implemented. Tighe says, "most people could relate to a previous project in some way, they knew somebody who had been on a previous project so that they could go and say 'what is a project issue report?' And users would also know, so they weren't learning good project management procedures at the same as we were trying to make big strides forward with the new system".

3.3.12 Participation

Clearly a highly participative approach to systems development was required to fit with the overall approach to the rebuilding of the LAS. One of the techniques employed was to have open forum sessions that anybody could attend. As Tighe recalls "We constantly sat down with team and non team members in forum type sessions where we pledged to answer any question as honestly as we could. We stood out at the front, as directors, and they gave us hell, but we shared as much as we could of what was going and our understandings. People wanted to know what was happening, what the view was on any topic, they wanted to know what would happen if you did this in this way and that went on a lot". There were a good number of these forum type sessions but in the end they became quite poorly attended, whereas initially the meetings would attract 30-40 people in the end only 2 or 3 were turning up. This was interpreted as success because it meant that people were happy, that they thought things were now being dealt with adequately and in the required depth.

As well as these forums a number of working groups or teams were established to discuss requirements, design procedures, forms, etc. For example, Hardy recalls the group meetings to have a first stab at designing what the new screens should look like. "A big group of us sat there with the systems people who made a first attempt... and we would say that we'd like it to look somewhat different and they would make some changes, there and then, so that we could actually see it. This was one of those exercises where we went full circle loads of times. But we'd all sit at the table with all the stakeholders and thrash things out until we were all happy with the end result and this went an awfully long way to convincing people that things were going to be different this time". Thus people who wanted to be involved would participate in the working groups whilst those that didn't want to be directly involved could attend the forums to hear what was happening and why.

3.3.13 Prototype approach

Essentially the approach adopted was that of prototyping and it was decided that the first part to be tackled would be the management of the resources, i.e. the ambulances, their locations and deployment. This seemed sensible as it would deliver important benefits. Armitage recalls, "So quite quietly I went away and produced the first prototype, not talking to users at all but having observed how the control room worked". Although it might seem strange not to talk to the users to begin with it was felt that a computer system was still such a contentious issue that it would be best to start with a prototype that they could see rather than asking them to provide a specification. The prototype was demonstrated to users and they said 'actually we'd like the computer to do the call-taking first, we're not so concerned about the resources. That can come later'. With a deep breath Tighe and Armitage agreed and went away to produce a call-taking prototype. Armitage thinks that this was an important decision, "I think to some extent it helped that we had gone down the wrong route and they said no, we want you to go over there, and we did. They saw that they could have considerable influence over the way we did things and that they weren't frightened to say, 'oh we don't like it like that, we want it changed'. Although it took time to build up it worked very well".

One technique that was used and worked quite successfully was the idea of 'competing prototypes'. So for example, at one stage four groups of dispatchers and call-takers were set off to design a part of the system and they each produced essentially the same functionality but in different ways. They would then discuss their work with the other groups and sometimes find that things had been missed or that there were better ways of doing things. As Tighe says "they started to close down and you could actually reach commonality and a consensus started to appear. You could actually get down to one version. You might have to say to group A 'I'm sorry but the other 3 groups think that actually this is the best way of doing it. Do you accept that?' and usually they would say yes...". This was found to be a good way of achieving consensus in this very difficult environment.

The rest of the development was undertaken using the prototyping approach, i.e. being non-prescriptive, very flexible, highly iterative. The users were not necessarily expected to come up with formal specifications, they could just react to prototypes. The idea was to bring the users on board and give them confidence again in the idea of computerisation and using a system. This fitted exactly with what the organisation was trying to achieve with the users slowly becoming interested in providing input.

The degree of flexibility and response to users comments and requests was amazing, particularly in the early stages. Clearly the system could have been developed much faster without this but it was deemed to be the over-riding consideration. Hardy suggests that this was very painful at times, "we would go full circle more often than not because you'd be presented with something and share it with the users. The users would mull it over and come up with all sorts of suggestions and then you'd come back again and review it. Quentin (Armitage) and Ian (Tighe) would make major changes and it would just go on and on and on like that. You would often come full circle and be back where you started, with what had originally been suggested. But unless you go through that process you don't feel like you've been involved". Armitage also remembers the frustration at times "we would tell them we've already changed this three times in different ways and we're now back to where we started - come on, please! However, if that happened, it was done deliberately, not through losing our cool, just to make them concentrate on it. We never lost our cool with them at all, although it may have appeared that we did, but that was for appearance sake".

3.4 Training

The training of users was a very important issue and indeed one that had been highlighted in the Page report as an area of weakness in the previous system. Although some training had taken place it was too early and by the time the system had been implemented the skills had been lost. This time a great deal of effort was devoted to training, not just on the computer system but training on all the procedures, both computer and manual. Part of the testing process was about gradually gaining the confidence of the users. Armitage states, "We did a stress related test on the system, for example, with some simulation, not full simulation, but some simulated keyboard input where we loaded the system up with 3000 jobs in an hour and at that time the busiest days were about 3000 jobs in the whole day. We let the users see this happen and they took heart by it, they saw the system working 25 times harder than it would ever need to and surviving". Hardy headed the training responsibility and she describes herself as the training 'stage manager'. She says "it was a very strange experience... to be asked the question 'how long do you need to train people?', it was an absolute luxury compared to the time before when it was what can we cram into the short time that we've got left". Indeed the need for full training was one reason why implementation was delayed. Tighe says "We weren't prepared to go live early… until we were all happy that the programs were fully tested, the system tested, integration tested and the users had tested and accepted and that we'd performance tested. We dug in on that one and said no."

3.5 Introduction of the new CAD system

The first part of the new computerised system, the call-taking, went live on 17th January 1996 and had thus taken around 18 months to develop and implement. After about a week of successful running the whole operation moved into the new control room (known as CAC, Central Ambulance Control). Subsequently various additional functionality was provided in February, July and September 1996 and indeed still continues, indicating the staged approach that was adopted with a little more added at each stage.

The system was by no means a full CAD system but was essentially a system to register calls and pass them to the dispatchers. It enabled the operators to receive a call and enter the details of an incident directly into the system. The computerised Gazetteer, using a Postal Address File, looked up the location and provided a map reference within one second. According to Armitage the Gazetteer hits over 97% of all locations in and around London. Once a valid address was established the details were routed to a screen in the appropriate sector desk for the controller to allocate a vehicle. The system provided the controller with information on which of the 150 or so deployment points around London was the nearest to the incident and the controller would then dispatch an appropriate ambulance. The system additionally provided the location of the nearest hospital for the controller to pass to the ambulance crew.

One of the most important enhancements of the basic system was that of 14th February 1996 which provided for the first time an element of re-engineering of the original manual process. This was the addition of 'early call viewing' for the controllers. Once the call takers had established the address of the incident that information was immediately available to the controllers to begin the dispatch process, i.e. before the call has finished. According to Armitage in the hour before the new software went in 38% of the calls were dispatched within 3 minutes, in the next hour it was 50%, and in the following hour 60%. An immediate and dramatic improvement that continued over the next few weeks to hit 80% and over the next few months 90%.

3.5.1 Success

The system was proving successful but this was not just a one-off effort. The improvements were sustained and Table 1 shows the annual performance measures. Although of course it should be remembered that it was not just the computer system but also all the other management, organisational and infrastructure changes, that contributed.

Year	**3 minute activation**	**8 minute response**	**14 minute response**
1993/94	35%	12%	62%
1994/95	36%	13%	68%
1995/96	44%	17%	76%
1996/97	80%	35%	90%
1997/98	85%	37%	91%
1998/99	89%	39%	87%

Table 1

The table shows significant improvements between 1995/6 and 1996/7 although some of the weeks in 1995/6 included the new system, so perhaps 1996/7 should really be compared with 1994/5 for a more accurate picture. This also needs to be viewed in the light of increasing demand for the service. For example, in 1996/97 the Service received 652,275 emergency 999 calls, an increase of 16% on the previous year. The improvements have been sustained and indeed continue to improve, although clearly not to the same degree.

In other terms it was a success too. People began to believe in the ability of IT to contribute to the LAS. As Armitage says, "although there were one or two people who were still skeptical, I think the majority had confidence. They wanted a computer system, to move away from their antiquated procedures. Now they're desperate for more. They keep clamouring, it's very rewarding". John Jenkins, one of the sector controllers, who was very critical of the previous management admits that, "there's no doubt about it, things really changed for the better. Gorham made a big impact on this Service and... improved it dramatically over the few years he was here". Hardy says that now people have "trust in the system, it very rarely goes wrong. It does what you want it to do, it's very simple to use, there's nothing complicated about it. That's quite comforting because you can feel confident that the next phase will be like that as well".

The public was also impressed. The number of complaints dropped quickly. According to Gorham they had been running at about a hundred complaints a month and in the course of about three months after the new system they were down to around 25 and below. The politicians were also impressed. The House of Commons Health Committee Report of December 1996 stated that they "were struck not only by the technological improvements but by the orderly and efficient atmosphere in the Central Ambulance Control. This contrasted strongly with the impression we had gained on our previous visit... which was of a Central Ambulance Control that was 'not a pleasant environment in which to work, being noisy, overcrowded and claustrophobic'". They go on to say "We warmly welcome the improvements in response times that the management and staff of the LAS have achieved... and the effective way in which new technology appears to have been introduced. We wish to congratulate both management and staff for their efforts in turning around an organisation which... was on 'the brink of collapse' only four years ago".

3.6 The future

The story of the new CAD system that won the award was thus essentially complete, although over time new elements of the system are still being added in a staged way. Prioritising calls, on a clinical basis, to ensure patients most in need (e.g. chest pains, cardiac arrest and severe trauma) receive the earliest possible attention will be a major feature of the system. Also making use of Calling Line Identity to extract a caller's address location automatically from an online BT database will save up to 40 seconds per call within the control room process. An AVLS (Automatic Vehicle Location System) is being implemented, providing real time information about what resources are available, where the ambulances are, what their status is, etc. hopefully enabling dispatchers assistance to do their job even better. As with all organisations there are still some on-going issues. Hardy, for example, highlights the relationship between operations and control which is still sometimes strained. People still talk about a 'them and us' situation and sometimes there is a bit of an atmosphere, although she thinks this is almost inevitable given the nature of the jobs that the two sides do. Others have suggested that some of the hard won lessons are easily forgotten and that some recent changes have been made too rapidly. Nevertheless compared to the past the future for the LAS looks very bright.

3.7 Lessons from LAS

Clearly each case is different and no two situations are really the same. Nevertheless there are perhaps some general lessons that might prove useful to a wider audience. It is hoped that some are clear from the above story but we would like to highlight the following.

Firstly, a clear lesson from the LAS is that no matter how bad things are, how many people are on your back, it is still possible to turn things around. As Gorham says, "There wasn't a day when I wasn't aware of the eye of the media on me. It certainly did not help but was only impossible if you allowed yourself to get trapped into thinking it was impossible, which was either that you were trying to do too many things at once, or you were trying to go at a pace that that was too fast". So belief is important, it can be done, although it may take time. In fact, it will definitely take time. As Hardy concluded "It took a long period of time, and we went very gently. There were no big bangs. There was no way we were going to introduce lots of things and expect people to be dealing with lots of new things, all at once. Whatever we do, we do things gradually now. That's the main lesson I think we learnt". Additionally there were no short cuts to be found, nobody was able to say that there was a trick or a magic solution and certainly no 'silver bullets'. Just a great deal of hard work.

The culture of an organisation is critically important. LAS had a culture of mistrust, a history of very poor industrial relations, a very damaging pay dispute, an antipathy towards computers, and a fear of management intentions. Gorham states that on his arrival he felt "that this was an organisation that didn't respect individuals", and he wanted to change that, "a lot of what I was trying to do was to restore that, together with a sense of direction". The problems were relatively easy to diagnose but very difficult to change. They key to the change was the acceptance that the staff essentially wanted to be able to do a good job. Therefore provide them with the capability of doing it. This meant finding out what they thought would improve things, get agreement, and deliver it successfully. Slowly, one step at a time, iterate until it is right. Have a strategy and a plan that you try and stick to but be flexible. Be prepared to change on the minor things but not on the major things. Adopt a very open, participative style of management. Involving people in a way that is more than just lip service takes time, you have to respond and incorporate their comments and ideas. It certainly takes much longer than issuing edicts. This would appear to be very sound advice, even in what might be perceived to be less alienated cultures. After all bringing staff, users, customers, etc. along and on board is always important.

In the LAS the decision not to be rushed, despite the very strong political pressures, was a critical decision. If one believes that the approach is right it is important not to be pushed into something else. Again we believe this has a wider relevance, we have seen too many managers buckle under pressure and hope for the best. For example, concerning implementation dates, we have known people agree to a date that they believe cannot be met.

Having the right people in place is clearly very important. The appointment of Gorham, as Chief Executive, was clearly a key part of the success. He was absolutely right for the situation. Everybody had good things to say for him and he was clearly exceptional in the circumstances. "When Martin Gorham was here, we tended to know what was going on. He was a lot more open than the management we had in the past". "People were very happy when Martin Gorham was here. He got things done, you knew what was going on, and he kept people informed".

His personality was obviously important, he went about his job with a "smile and a sense of humour", he was good at dealing with people. He adopted a very open style of management. He led by example and he was a "role-model" and encouraged others to adopt the same attitudes. He, of course, says that he had a good team, which is obviously correct but as we have seen he built that team. He spent a lot of time and effort recruiting the right people, with the right attitudes and experience. On the IT side Tighe and Armitage were crucial. For those already in-post he invested heavily in management development and training. So getting the right team is not accidental but is probably the most important element in a successful project.

Adequate resources were also clearly key to the turnaround of the LAS. The 'warm-up' projects involved the expenditure of large scale resources. The turnaround could probably not have been achieved without this investment. In some ways Gorham was lucky that the crash and its political impact together with the various government reports helped to loosen the purse strings. Although the reality was that the Service had probably been under funded for many years and this was just redressing the balance. Nevertheless it is obvious that turnaround projects cost money and that without significant investment success would not have occurred. Too many Chief Executives think that such critical change projects can be done on the cheap. Of course investment is a necessary factor although not a sufficient one. A crisis of some kind is occasionally good for shaking up an organisation's thinking and freeing up resources. However, although it may have had some beneficial effects in terms of resources in this case it was clearly not a price worth paying.

3.8 Development level

In relation to systems development lessons there are a number that can be highlighted. However, and it is a lesson in itself, the general managerial and development issues are closely intertwined. The IT function was highly integrated with the business, both in a physical and a conceptual sense. Gorham states, "IT was an absolutely essential function and it was vital that we integrated our approach to IT with our whole approach to people management in general, it couldn't be anything else. If it had been we would have failed". Also for the approach to work the IT people had to be on hand and on site. Had they been located in some other building or part of the country, as is the case with some IT departments, it almost certainly would not have worked as well. They were seen not just as the IT department but as an essential and integrated part of the business. It has been shown how they did this by building credibility through various 'warm-up' projects, not all of which were IT based.

Although LAS saw the CAD system as important it was very clearly just the last step in the jigsaw and was dealt with in the same way as any non-IT based project. The management approach was just the same and the people were the same. A participative/prototyping approach to development was adopted that did not just address the computer part but included the whole business system, including the integration of the manual procedures. The participation of the users and stakeholders in the development was crucial if, as has been seen, sometimes frustrating for the developers themselves.

One further element of the system itself worth highlighting is the recognition of the degree of intelligence and experience that the users have and apply (in this case controllers and dispatchers) in the operation of such a system. When things are out of the ordinary they apply judgement. For example, if an incident occurred in outer London and the nearest available ambulance was some distance away the controller might contact the neighbouring ambulance service and see if they had a closer vehicle. The old CAD system did not recognise this kind of behaviour and indeed actually prevented it. The new one enabled the controller to undertake this kind of thing as the system was flexible enough.

Again, as for the rest of the business, the people were key. The appointment of the IT Director, Ian Tighe, was very important. Gorham knew relatively little about computing and IT himself but he made sure that the person appointed did but in addition he made sure they could explain and discuss the technical issues with non-technical people in the business in a convincing way. They had to be good on both sides, technology and management, including dealing with people. Gorham instinctively appointed someone who was a hybrid manager, i.e. someone who was skilled and comfortable with both the business and the IT roles. Tighe, in turn, continued this approach with his appointment of Armitage. Apart from their hybrid skills both Tighe and Armitage had substantial experience with command and control system in the West Midlands Police. They both had confidence in their abilities to deliver on the technical side because they had the experience of having done it before. A very important aspect particularly in the light of the lack of experience of the previous system developers.

Tighe and Armitage were the only two IT people involved in the whole development, with Armitage undertaking the majority of the programming development. A surprisingly small team, particularly given the wide ranging nature of their roles. However, in IT development small is very effective, as long as the people are good. There is a well known 'law' that suggests that the more people involved in development the longer it takes, and that adding extra bodies to a late running IT project makes it even later. The LAS seemed to get this element right.

A further lesson, and one that is often stressed, but certainly well worth emphasising, is the importance of testing. Both system testing and business testing, i.e. making sure it all works together. Testing helps to ensure it all works on a normal day but also that it will still work on exceptional days. More than that testing is about understanding what happens when something does go wrong. What happens when the back-up system is activated. Does it work? Does everyone know what they should be doing? Testing to ensure not only that it works but that people are confident that it will work. Unfortunately, testing frequently gets squeezed because it is one of the last things that are undertaken. Any slippage in the overall time-scale and the only area where time can be made up is the testing. Clearly it is never right to fall into that trap, even in less safety critical systems than that of the LAS. Much better in the long run to bite the bullet and extend the deadline, even if it might be embarrassing for some.

3.9 References

[1] Beynon-Davies, P. (1995) Information Systems 'Failure': The Case of the London Ambulance Service's Computer Aided Despatch Project, European Journal of Information Systems, 4, pp171-184.

[2] Collins, T. (1997) (with Bicknell, D.) *Crash: Ten Easy Ways to Avoid a Computer Disaster*, Simon and Schuster, London.

[3] Finkelstein, A. & Dowell, J. (1996) *A Comedy of Errors: the London Ambulance Service case study*, in Proceedings 8th International Workshop on Software Specification & Design IWSSD-8, (IEEE CS Press), 1996, 2-4.

[4] The Guardian (1992), 'AMBULANCE CHIEF RESIGNS, 29th November, P1-2.

[5] The Independent (1992), 'SOFTWARE FAILURE MAY BE BEHIND AMBULANCE CRISIS' by Susan Watts and Ian McKinnon, 30th October 1992, P2.

[6] Page, D., Williams, P. and Boyd, D. (1993) *Report of the Public Inquiry into the London Ambulance Service*, HMSO, London.

An Overview – The Final Analysis

A good starting point

Few organisations in today's economic climate believe they can operate successfully without the support of an IS/IT system. There have been some spectacular IS/IT failures, and the popular press, in the UK at least, delights in recounting the millions of pounds spent on systems which have either never been used, or which have failed to deliver the benefits that organisations believed possible. Despite the high failure rate, organisations seem only too eager to spend an enormous amount of their budget on IS/IT systems. Although in recognition of the costs involved, both in monetary terms but also more generally for the business, organisations are now adopting a more cautious approach to such development. It is therefore timely that literature reflects not only the failures in IS/IT systems development but also the very many success stories; as in life more generally, there are valuable lessons to be learned not only from doing things badly but also from doing them well. To this end, we have presented and described three UK-based case studies, drawing from them some tentative conclusions as to the factors involved in successful IS/IT systems development. However, there is a tendency in work such as this to seek or describe experiences that, it is hoped, will lead to the creation of a list of 'ten tips for a successful IS/IT system'. As the evidence presented from these case studies shows, success cannot be so easily explained, and indeed such an approach should be resisted. Change, and the management of change, is highly complex and involves different people, doing different tasks, in different contexts and at different times. There is, then, no simple recipe for success, but the case studies presented here serve to raise awareness of the factors involved; a good starting point for better understanding complexity in IS/IT development surely.

Managing change – understanding the business context

Central to the success of any new system is both understanding, and managing, change. This change necessarily involves changing the physical systems themselves but also, and crucially, involves the management of people's expectations. This is not to undermine the importance of technology; indeed, inherent in the notion of a successful system is that everything 'works'. Yet many of the reported failures of IS/IT systems recount that the technology 'worked' very well indeed, which raises the vital issue of what is understood by the term 'information system'. Although it necessarily includes the technology, and that it must 'work', these case studies illustrate that it is vital to look beyond the merely technical and to encompass the human perspective. The three case studies presented report on the development of information systems in three very different business contexts. One is the work of the London Ambulance Service, where change (and risk) is, quite literally, a matter of life or death. The second is in the world of finance, namely share-dealing at the Halifax Building Society. The third, the work of the AA, an organisation which assists motorists when their vehicles have broken down.

Although these are very different contexts indeed, and the way in which each achieved its success was naturally different, it highlights a factor which is perhaps the most important aspect of IS/IT success, that is, the value of understanding the business context. Although this necessarily involves external factors such as competition within the industry and political and social issues more generally, those involved in managing change need to take a long, hard look at their own organisation, or culture. As the case studies show the context influences (and should influence) the way the system is developed. Thus, in the case of the London Ambulance Service the new system had to be introduced slowly as trust had to be built up through a number of smaller projects. As a general rule, a phased development and implementation is usually safer, leading to fewer problems during the final implementation. This is of course not always possible, and indeed external circumstances dictated that the Halifax Building Society roll-over had to be a 'big bang', that is, they had to implement the system to serve all customers at once.

IT in harmony with the business needs

Another of the major success factors, evident in all three cases, is that the system should be driven by the needs of the business more generally and also how important it is for IT to be integrated within this. In the case of the London Ambulance Service and AA Help, IT teams were not only physically located together but they were in constant contact with those more involved on the business side of the organisation. Firstly, however, there needs to be a vision of where the business needs to be, or needs to be going, in the future. Having identified this, it is then time to explore how, or how far, that vision can be technically implemented. An holistic view should be adopted, where the needs of the organisation more generally are addressed. This will necessarily involve analysis of the organisation itself, how open or resistant the people within it are to change and how technology can support that change. Although almost everyone in any organisation is keen to stress that they want and need change, the reality is that most people, and organisations, are extremely reluctant to take the risk associated with changing behaviour and systems. Identifying whether the organisation is ready for change, and how much change, is thus a key concept that needs to be explored. Another issue related to this is deciding whether the new information system should be designed to mirror previous, paper-based procedures or should instead result in the re-designing of work processes. Testing is highlighted as a way of reducing risk and is thus a vital ingredient of success. In the case of the Halifax Building Society, system errors would have been absolutely disastrous given that it had to function effectively from the very first moment. However, even in the case of AA Help, where the old system was there as a back-up, the introduction of a new system that had major faults would have had negative effects not only on the business but also on staff morale. It is better to extend the deadline (if possible), rather than introduce an untested system. In the case of the AA and the Halifax Building Society the culture of these organisations was open to change, or perhaps more accurately, at least not adverse to change. This meant that the information systems introduced could change working practices and that they were not actively opposed, either overtly or covertly. The case study of the London Ambulance Service illustrates that in an organisation with, among other factors, a culture of resistance, a high level of discontent and with the recent history of a disastrous IS/IT system still fresh in the minds of many, change needed to be introduced slowly and cautiously.

User Confidence

In order to increase user confidence at the London Ambulance Service, the initial computerised system was very much based on the paper one and only at the later stage were some changes to work procedures introduced. Managing change was therefore a particularly difficult task, and it required a lot of negotiation and user involvement. Indeed, user involvement is a key factor in success according to the evidence from the case studies here. In each organisation users were asked to participate in the systems development and their views were sought even when it might be argued that there was perhaps not a need for them. That is, even when the developers were sure what was needed, users were constantly consulted. It is clearly seen as important that users need to be co-opted in the process and ultimately that they feel that they own the system, that is, that they do not feel that it is something that has been imposed on them by 'others'. This message is perhaps best demonstrated by the views expressed by those at the AA. User participation helps not only to co-opt the people but should lead to a system that better reflects users' needs and ultimately that is more likely to be used by them to its full potential. How can we ensure that the change process is managed well and that ultimately the project is successful in terms of the organisational fit of the new information system and the software produced? This last point, about users, draws attention to what is identified in each case study as the most important factor of all; people, and at all levels of the organisation.

People

People, supported by right procedures (and not a little luck) can make the project work. Thus, continuous commitment from the top managers has to be secured and the right people appointed to key posts. Equally important is to ensure that users take ownership of the system, that they have part in its development, that they understand its aims and are told how it will affect them; training is therefore essential. It is clearly a challenge for any company to recognise and to retain good employees, and although financial rewards are important, they are not sufficient. Making people feel appreciated and involved in what they do (giving them ownership of their tasks however large or small) encourages them to stay with the organisation. Project management methodologies are, as the case studies demonstrate, useful tools, although they afford different degrees of flexibility. However, project management together with systems analysis and development methodologies can only contribute to success if the right people are there in the first place. In terms of system's development it is again clear that the choice of people is vital. The development team does not have to be large (in fact often smaller teams work better) but it has to include some highly skilled core people. Although a mix of skills is required, it is vital that this includes the ability to communicate well with users. Working in a team, and building a team spirit, as well as taking personal responsibility are key for those involved in the development of a successful IS/IT system. What is an enduring dilemma for all organisations is how to ensure that the 'right' people are in place. As discussed earlier, change, and the management of change, is highly complex. The development of each IS/IT system involves a unique blend of different people, doing different tasks, in different contexts and at different times. Thus the 'right' people involved in developing a certain IS/IT system might turn out to be the 'wrong' people for what might appear to be a similar project in a different organisation at another time. Although this is no doubt a worry for those who fear change and uncertainty, those (few) who drive or lead change will in contrast view managing the complexities in IS/IT systems development in a changing world as a fascinating challenge. Whatever your own view on change, the case studies presented here describe how this has very successfully been managed in three large organisations and will, it is hoped, offer a fresh perspective on IS/IT development.